A GENERAL INTRODUCTION to the NEW TESTAMENT

James A. Borland, Th.D.

Professor of New Testament and Theology
Liberty Baptist Theological Seminary
Liberty University

D1531129

UNIVERSITY BOOK HOUSE
Lynchburg, Virginia

Original © 1986
Revised © 1989
Newly Revised © 1995
4th Revised Edition © 2008
UNIVERSITY BOOK HOUSE
200 Russell Woods Drive
Lynchburg, Virginia 24502

Borland, James A.   1944--
    A General Introduction to the New Testament
    Bibliographies included
    Includes indexes

ISBN 9780-936461-05-2

Printed in the United States of America

To Linda
My sweet, lovely, precious, adorable wife,
My closest friend and ever faithful help meet,
Who provides me with great joy, companionship,
Spiritual fellowship, and the tastiest and best meals
Anyone on earth has ever consumed,

AND

To our many, many lovely Grandchildren
Jordan
Micah
Christopher
Gabrielle
Claire
Ava
Nathanael
Abigail
Samuel
Malachi
Cody
Christian
Perry
Landon
Lacee

ACKNOWLEDGEMENTS

I want to express my sincere thanks to the many who helped make this volume a reality. I thank God for the late Marchant King (1903-1985) who demonstrated to me a love for the Lord Jesus Christ who is *the* theme of the New Testament. I acknowledge my many students who encouraged me for years to place this material in printed form to ease their note taking tasks! My colleagues Dick Patterson, Daniel Kim, and Dick Bohrer also urged me to write.

The original manuscript was carefully and cheerfully typed by Charlotte Waggoner who offered helpful suggestions in the process. I am greatly indebted to her. My hand-drawn charts were placed in a computer by my friend Laurice Jennings, and two have been redone by my son-in-law, Chuck Gammon. In the final proof-reading I was assisted by a top-notch "Intro" student, Beverly Edmondson, who gave unsparingly of her time and expertise.

The manuscript was also read in its first draft format by a select group of more than thirty students who offered suggestions and pointed out flaws. I thank each of them, but wish especially to acknowledge Mike Amos, Patrick Barrett, Rev. Jeff Crabtree, David Druckenmiller, Donny Hargett, Joseph Pak, Jeong-Kun Park, Kyung-Il Park, Chung-Deak Moon, Bob Remaily, Kevin Stephens, Mickey Stephens, Sheila Suders, and Andy Zivojinovic.

Mr. Bill James, Keith Robinson, and Rhonda Cash were of special assistance in helping prepare this book for initial publication. Keith also did the cover. The 4th Revised Edition has expanded and updated the bibliographies, and updated other information. All blame for the actual typesetting must be borne by the author, but it was exciting to learn and do something new.

James Allen Borland
Lynchburg, Virginia
November 9, 2007

CONTENTS

PART ONE:

GENERAL BACKGROUND

PART TWO

THE CANON AND TEXT

v

LIST OF ILLUSTRATIONS

PREFACE

My first "Introduction to the New Testament" in an official way was gained from Marchant King (1903-1985), who taught a course with that title in the spring of 1965. That and a cults class were the most theologically beneficial and biblically enlightening situations I took part in that semester. My understanding of the New Testament was multiplied many times over by what I learned in those brief lectures. I had a fair grasp of the stories and contents of the New Testament, but the individual pieces of the puzzle, as well as many pieces I had missed, finally were brought together.

So impressed was I by the textbook for that course, Henry Thiessen's *Introduction to the New Testament,* that I have used it myself in teaching the course for many years. However, I found myself increasingly supplementing that good book with many lectures to fill in important areas of **background** as well as items of practical interest to most students. The pages that follow are not meant to rival the depth of Zahn's three volumes or Guthrie's 1000+ page tome. My purpose is not to interact with the latest critical opinion or to refute every heretical viewpoint, although there is a place for that. The materials presented herein are meant to be simple and brief, but practical and informative.

The book falls into two parts: I. *General Background,* chapters 1-9; and II. *The Canon and Text,* chapters 10-15. Except for an *Appendix* on the Synoptic Problem, matters of special introduction have been left for a future volume. The textbook format may facilitate classroom use as well as an organized presentation and viewing of the materials. The graphics are given with the knowledge that one picture is worth a thousand words. The review and discussion sections may be used individually or within a group setting, and the *bibliographies* with each chapter suggest where further studies may be pursued by interested readers. Since I have always appreciated a book with indexes, several are included with this volume.

James A. Borland
Lynchburg, Virginia
January, 1986

PREFACE TO THE REVISED EDITION

I am pleased that this volume was received well and provided a measure of help to its readers. I thank those who made suggestions for changes and corrections--some of which have been incorporated into this revision. A special thanks goes to Jerry W. Scheidbach, pastor of Wells Road Baptist Church in Ventura, California, for his careful and insightful comments.

James A. Borland
Lynchburg, Virginia
January, 1989

PART ONE

GENERAL
BACKGROUND

1

WHAT IS NEW TESTAMENT INTRODUCTION?

I. LOOKING AT THE OVERALL PICTURE

God is a big subject. He is not only the creator and sustainer of the entire universe and of man, but He is also the revealer of any knowledge man may obtain about God. This knowledge about God is called revelation and falls generally into two categories. General revelation is that which all men can see and learn from the creation itself-- that God is great and powerful. Special revelation concerns God entrusting to certain individuals some of the knowledge about Himself and His creation. This has come through dreams and visions (Gen 20:3-7; Matt 1:20-25), God's voice from heaven (Gen 22:11; Matt 17:5; John 12:28), Old Testament appearances of Christ in human form,[1] the incarnation of Christ (Gal 4:4), and by means of God's Spirit speaking to men's hearts (2 Tim 3:16; 2 Pet 1:21).

---

[1]See my book *Christ in the Old Testament* (Fearn, Scotland: Christian Focus, 1995), 184 pp which thoroughly treats this subject. Copies may be secured from University Book House, 200 Russell Woods Drive, Lynchburg, VA 24502, USA.

The subject matter of New Testament Introduction is that part of God's special revelation known as the New Testament. In order to properly understand it, several realms of study suggest themselves--including the Greek language, the canon, inspiration, textual criticism, hermeneutics, exegesis, history, geography, and archaeology. It could encompass an entire encyclopedia of knowledge to unlock the treasures of the New Testament. In fact, a sample Theological Encyclopedia is offered below to show at a glance where the areas of Introduction fit into the overall picture of study. The encyclopedia of all knowledge about God falls under four major headings: (1) Exegetical Theology; (2) Historical Theology; (3) Systematic Theology; and (4) Practical Theology. Theology means the study of God, from *theos*=God, and *logos*=word. The entire area preceded by the asterisks is generally included in New Testament Introduction.

THE THEOLOGICAL ENCYCLOPEDIA

I. Exegetical Theology
  A. Biblical Languages
**B. The Canon and Its Parts
    1. Canonics--which books are to be included
    2. Isagogics--all preliminary questions about authorship, date, integrity, genuineness, etc.
  C. The Text and Its Interpretation
    1. Textual Criticism
    2. Hermeneutics
    3. Exegesis

D. The Content of Revelation
   1. Biblical History
   2. Biblical Archaeology
   3. Biblical Theology

II. Historical Theology
A. Ancient Church History, A.D. 30-500
B. Medieval Church History, A.D. 500-1500
C. Modern Church History,
   A.D. 1500-Present

III. Systematic Theology
A. Dogmatic Theology
   1. History of Doctrine
   2. Systematic Theology--Theology
      Proper, Anthropology, Christology,
      Soteriology, Ecclesiology,
      Eschatology
B. Ethics (Principles and Application)
C. Apologetics
   1. Christian Theism (Philosophical)
   2. Comparative Religions
   3. Polemics (Doctrines)

IV. Practical Theology
A. Missions and Evangelism
B. Christian Education
C. Promotion of Spiritual Life
   1. Worship and Prayer
   2. Homiletics
   3. Pastoral Theology

The areas considered in an introduction to the New Testament are generally limited to the area preceded by the asterisks. The next section attempts to explain just what is incorporated within the fields of canonics and isagogics.

II. NARROWING THE DEFINITION

The all-purpose word "introduction" really includes a study of those items that must be considered *before* a proper exposition of the Bible can begin. That is the meaning of the term isagogics. Initially, it is important to understand which books make up the true canon of Scripture, and why. Inspiration is also a preliminary question, as is the matter of textual criticism (also called lower criticism). Those subjects in general are included under the heading of **general introduction.**

Areas that concern each particular book are included in **special introduction.** These are such topics as authorship, composition, date, genuineness, purpose, and other critical questions regarding each book of the New Testament. These matters are referred to as higher criticism. The term higher criticism is neutral and need not imply any liberal bias.

III. SHARPENING THE FOCUS

Part One--General Background--deals with special matters of importance that are also preliminary to understanding much of the New Testament revelation. The New Testament did not appear suddenly in a hermetically sealed vacuum, but was the outcome of miraculous events that occurred around the first century of our era. What that world was like is important for us to know--at least in an elementary fashion. That is the purpose of Part One. Thus, it includes a brief historical background of the New Testament, some comments on the geography of Palestine, the story of Herod and his family, a treatment of

Jewish and Christian apocryphal literature, the
Jewish sects and parties, as well as keys to
understanding New Testament chronology and
archaeology.

The author has found that an adequate
treatment of these items of general background is
not usually found in most texts available for New
Testament Introduction.[2] Yet students invariably
comment that lectures and discussion of the issues
of general background were most interesting and
enlightening and proved to be of inestimable
worth when it came to fitting the New Testament
into one's frame of reference. The following pages
are intended to *expand* the reader's frame of
reference regarding the New Testament, yet in a
way that is neither pedantic nor overly technical.

As one can see from the table of the contents
matters of general introduction are covered in
Part Two--The Canon and Text, chapters 10-15.
The synoptic problem, although actually a part of
special introduction, is felt to be important enough
to merit treatment in the Appendix of this volume.

IV. GRASPING THE EFFECT OF PRESUPPOSITIONS

A. What Is a Presupposition?

Presuppositions affect the way people view the
world around them. A presupposition is
something that one accepts as a fact and presumes
to be true, whether it is in fact true or not. It
naturally follows that some presuppositions are
no doubt wrong, while others are indeed correct.
Presuppositions are frequently based on prior

---

[2]This includes such well-known works as Guthrie, Harrison, Hiebert,
Kümmel, McNeile, and Thiessen.

opinion or knowledge one may possess about someone or something.

B. Presuppositions About God and the Bible

For purposes of this study one's presuppositions about God and the Bible are all-important. If one is a naturalist, atheist, evolutionist, or anti-supernaturalist, his view of God, the Bible, and the events recorded therein will be colored by his philosophical presuppositions. On the other hand, if one believes (presumes) that God exists and has certain attributes, and that the Bible is His inerrant revelation to mankind, then his view of the events in the Bible will differ remarkably from that of the naturalist.

1.   *The Naturalist and the Bible.* For the naturalist, there is no God--only eternal matter that somehow formed itself into the earth and the universe that man presently observes. Many liberal biblical scholars accept the naturalist presupposition. As a consequence, all biblical and other religious explanations of God, creation, sin, and salvation must be false--since there is no God, at least to them. The Bible then becomes the religious thought of the Jews as it evolved over many centuries. What of the miracles? According to this point of view, the miracles were stories, just like other myths, legends, or fables. Jesus, to them, may have been a great moral teacher, but He could not have been "God."

This viewpoint is somewhat at odds with morality. If there is no God, and all happened by chance, then there are no absolutes. There can be no such thing as morality, either good or bad. Jesus was either liar, lunatic, or Lord. Since He could not be Lord, for the naturalist, He should be labeled plainly as liar or lunatic, or both. If Jesus was not God as He claimed and as men understood Him to claim (Mark 2:7-11; John 5:18; 10:30-33), then He was certainly a bold deceiver--promising men eternal life or eternal damnation based on how they received Him (John 3:36).

The liberal naturalistic critic seeks to explain everything he finds in the Bible in accordance with his naturalistic presuppositions. Heaven and hell are myths or mere earthly states of mind. All prophecy is rejected as impossible. The dates of books containing "prophecy" are pushed ahead until after the events have transpired. The reputed authorship of biblical books is questioned, and often rejected. To the naturalist, the Bible is nothing more than a human book composed by fallible human authors who were creatures of their time and who made plenty of obvious mistakes and contradictions galore!

2. *The Neo-Orthodox and the Bible.* The Neo-Orthodox scholars, beginning with the German Karl Barth, reacted to the bold-faced liberalism, naturalism, and historicism of the later 19th and early 20th centuries. Espousing a "new orthodoxy," they claimed that God, the miraculous, and the Bible were real--but that they existed in a realm that was *above* our historical, fact-verifying world. God acted in salvation history (*heilsgeschichte*). Barth and his followers tried to wed biblical revelation with existentialist philosophy. The result has been a quagmire of double-talk, paradox, inconsistency, and absurdity.

3. *The Fundamentalist and the Bible.* The Biblicist, or Fundamentalist, has as his first presupposition that the Bible is the Word of the living God--and that as God gave it, it was 100%

true, accurate, and reliable in whatever it said. The Fundamentalist is not afraid to say that the Bible as written down by men was plenarily verbally inspired, and inerrant in all matters, including geography, history, science, morality, and so forth. These presuppositions are taken from the Bible itself. Thus, if it says that Paul wrote the Pastoral Epistles (1 Tim 1:1; Tit 1:1; 2 Tim 1:1), or that Peter was the author of 2 Peter (2 Pet 1:1; 3:1), the Biblicist believes it. If it says Jesus predicted the fall of Jerusalem and the destruction of its great Herodian temple (Luke 21:24;Matt 24), the Fundamentalist accepts that as truth. If Jesus claimed that He was the *only* way to heaven (John 14:6), then all other religions or "ways to heaven" must be false.

There are no errors, mistakes, or contradictions in the Bible either. A joke is told about a man who just knew he had discovered an impossible statement when he came to Josh 3 which told of a few priests carrying the ark across the Jordan River. He knew that Gen 6 said the ark was over 450 feet long, 75 feet wide, and 45 feet tall! He was guilty of *confusing* Scripture with Scripture instead of *comparing* Scripture with Scripture.

In conclusion, presuppositions greatly affect the way we view the Bible. This writer approaches the Bible with the firm convictions of a Fundamentalist, and with the fervent hope that those who follow this study will do so as well.

V. FOR REVIEW AND DISCUSSION

1.   How does New Testament introduction fit into the overall picture of the knowledge about God?

2. What are the four areas listed in the Theological Encyclopedia, and with what does each deal?

3. What are some of the main concerns of New Testament introduction?

4. Distinguish between general and special introduction.

5. How will this textbook differ from many others in the material and subjects treated? Do you feel that this will be helpful?

6. What effect do presuppositions have on one's approach to the Bible? Explain.

7. Define and discuss the three presuppositional viewpoints mentioned in section IV. Have you read any books or talked with persons who held a naturalistic or Neo-Orthodox viewpoint? What was your reaction?

8. From where do the presuppositions the Fundamentalist holds about God and the Bible come? How big of a difference do these presuppositions make?

9. Are there any errors, mistakes, or contradictions in the Bible? Explain.

VI.   FOR FURTHER READING AND RESEARCH

Archer, Gleason Leonard. *New International Encyclopedia of Bible Difficulties Based on the NIV and the NASB.* Grand Rapids: Zondervan, 1998. 476 pp.

Boa, Kenneth, and Robert M. Bowman. *Faith Has Its Reasons An Integrative Approach to Defending Christianity : an Apologetics Handbook.* Colorado Springs: NavPress, 2001.

Carson, D. A., and Douglas J. Moo. *An Introduction to the New Testament.* Grand Rapids: Zondervan, 2005.

12   *A General Introduction to the New Testament*

Campbell-Jack, Walter Campbell, Gavin McGrath, and C. Stephen Evans. *New Dictionary of Christian Apologetics.* Leicester, England: Inter-Varsity Press, 2006. xx + 779.

Dobson, Ed, Jerry Falwell, and Edward E. Hindson. *The Fundamentalist Phenomenon The Resurgence of Conservative Christianity.* Garden City, NY: Doubleday, 1981. xvi + 270.

Dockery, David S., K. A. Mathews, and Robert Bryan Sloan. *Foundations for Biblical Interpretation.* Nashville: Broadman & Holman, 1994.

Geisler, Norman L. *Baker Encyclopedia of Christian Apologetics.* Grand Rapids: Baker Books, 1999.

Köstenberger, Andreas J., ed. *Whatever Happened to Truth?* Wheaton, IL: Crossway Books, 2005. 173 pp.

Lindsell, Harold. *The Battle for the Bible.* Grand Rapids: Zondervan, 1976. 218 pp.

Machen, J. Gresham. *Christianity and Liberalism.* New York: Macmillan, 1923. 189 pp.

_____. *The Christian Faith in the Modern World.* New York: Macmillan, 1936. x + 258.

Marshall, I. Howard, Kevin J. Vanhoozer, and Stanley E. Porter. *Beyond the Bible Moving from Scripture to Theology.* Grand Rapids: Baker Academic, 2004. 136 pp.

Thiessen, Henry Clarence. *Introduction to the New Testament.* Grand Rapids: Eerdmans, 1943. pp. xi-xx.

Tulga, Chester E. *The Case Against Modernism.* Chicago: Conservative Baptist Fellowship, 1949. 61 pp.

Van Til, Cornelius. *The Reformed Pastor and the Defense of Christianity & My Credo.* Philipsburg, NJ: Presbyterian and Reformed, 1980. 93 pp.

2

A BRIEF HISTORICAL BACKGROUND OF THE NEW TESTAMENT

I. INTRODUCTION

The New Testament writings cannot be isolated from the rest of the history of mankind. The events that centered around the birth, life, death and resurrection of Jesus Christ are intimately tied to the *land* of Palestine during the first century A.D. The apostolic proclamation of the meaning of Christ's ministry, vicarious death, and triumphant resurrection and ascension spread throughout the *Roman world* touching many, if not all, of the approximately thirty provinces of that empire.

But the New Testament contains not only *geographical, political,* and *historical* connections with the first century world, but also a vital *racial* dimension. The fact must not be ignored that Jesus was a Jewish messiah sent "to redeem those who were under the law" (Gal 4:5). The background and history of the Jewish people must therefore be understood before one can truly comprehend the meaning of the New Testament. Furthermore, the writings of the new covenant claim to be a fulfillment of the prophecies of the

Old Testament. The mention of such personages as Abraham, Isaac, Jacob, Moses, David, and Elijah presupposes that the reader knows who they are. So some historical background of the Children of Israel is in order.

II. BASIC OLD TESTAMENT DATES

A friend of mine who seeks to bring Jewish people to a saving knowledge of Christ was once asked this question by a Jewish lady. In all sincerity she asked, "Was Jesus before or after Abraham?" She actually did not know. In an effort to lend some historical perspective, the list that follows gives some important personages and events with their approximate dates. It is good to have them well in mind as fixed points of reference.

Abraham	2000 B.C.
Moses	1500 B.C.
The Exodus	1445 B.C.
David	1000 B.C.
Solomon's Death (Divided Kingdom Begins)	931 B.C.
Samaria Falls	722 B.C.
Judah Falls	606 B.C.
Solomon's Temple Destroyed	586 B.C.
Judah Returns from Exile	536 B.C.
Zerubbabel's Temple Dedicated	516 B.C.
Ezra and Nehemiah	444 B.C.
Malachi	435 B.C.

————————————————————

(End of Old Testament)

————————————————————

Alexander the Great	333 B.C.
The Maccabean Revolt	167 B.C.

Herod Appointed King of Jews   40 B.C.
Death of Herod   4 B.C.

As one can readily see, the Old Testament closes with Malachi, yet the stage was continuously being set for the New Testament during the next 400 years. That period between 400 B.C. and the birth of Christ has been the subject of numerous books--many with quite descriptive titles such as Harry Ironside's *The Four Hundred Silent Years;* William Fairweather's *From the Exile to the Advent;* R. Wadi Moss' *From Malachi to Matthew;* D. S. Russell's *Between the Testaments;* Werner Foerster's *From the Exile to Christ;* and many others. Their purpose is to fill in the gap of time that separates the close of the Old Testament and the opening of the pages of the New Testament.

III. DANIEL AND THE FOUR KINGDOMS

A basic historical outline of the kingdoms that would fill the gap between the exile of Israel and the advent of Christ was provided in the prophecy of Daniel in the 6th century B.C. The key chapters to examine are Dan 2 and 7 which run parallel in giving an account of these four kingdoms. These familiar prophetic portions suggest that four successive empires would hold sway over the middle east from the time of Daniel (605 B.C.) to the first coming of Messiah the Prince (Dan 9:24-27).

A. DANIEL 2

Daniel relates that Nebuchadnezzar, the king of Babylon and the Chaldean empire, had a troubling dream in the second year of his reign. He saw a majestic human-like figure smashed by a huge stone which then filled the entire earth (Dan 2:31-35). The figure in the dream was composed of four parts: a gold head, silver breast and arms, bronze belly and thighs, and legs of iron, but the feet of which were iron mixed with clay.

Interestingly enough, the image was quite top-heavy. Gold is much heavier than silver. Silver weighs more than brass, and iron is also lighter than brass. The image was also more valuable from top to bottom! The suggestion of successively deteriorating kingdoms may be hinted here.

Daniel explained the dream to the king (Dan 2:36-45). The golden head stood for Nebuchadnezzar and his kingdom (v. 38, "you are this head of gold"). The silver represented a second kingdom which Daniel described as "inferior to" that of Nebuchadnezzar's Chaldean empire (v. 39). The second kingdom was to be followed by a third "which shall rule over all the earth" (v. 39). The fourth kingdom, the iron legs and feet, became divided (v. 41), and was smashed by the rock which filled the earth (v. 44). The rock stands for the kingdom which "the God of heaven will set up" (v. 44).

Most conservative biblical scholars believe the four kingdoms predicted by Daniel were (1) Babylon, (2) Medo-Persia, (3) Greece, and (4) Rome. Some critical scholars attempt to make the Medes second, the Persians third, and the Greeks fourth--leaving out Rome entirely. This is done frequently in an effort to rid Daniel of the element of true *predictive* prophecy, and flies in the face of the historical evidence as well. Dan 8:20-21 clearly indicate that Daniel considered the Medes and Persians to be one united kingdom that was succeeded by the Grecian empire.

B. Daniel 7

In Daniel 7 four beasts are seen to be struggling for progressive mastery over the earth (v. 3). The first was a lion (v. 4), followed by a bear (v. 5), which was succeeded by a four-winged leopard (v. 6). After the leopard came a "dreadful and terrible . . . diverse" beast (v.7). Without going into great detail, Daniel indicated that the four beasts represented four kings (v. 17), or kingdoms (v.23), which successively would bear rule on earth, followed by the kingdom of God (v. 22, 27). These beasts likewise stand for (1) Babylon, (2) Medo-Persia, (3) Greece, and (4) Rome.

Through Daniel, God was allowing His people Israel to have a glimpse into the future--into that period we call the 400 silent years that bridge the gap between the Old and New Testaments.

C. Daniel 8

Dan 8 predicts the conflicts between the second and third kingdoms mentioned in Dan 2 and 7--Medo-Persia and Greece. Pictured as a ram, Medo-Persia comes from the east (v. 4), but was suddenly destroyed by a great he-goat from the west (v. 5-7), which was Greece (v. 20-21). The reason for detailing this struggle and what followed was to reassure Israel of final victory over the wicked ruler Antiochus IV, called Epiphanes (v. 23-25). After Alexander the Great's untimely death (323 B.C.), struggles ensued which eventually resulted in four consolidations of his divided Greek empire by around 300 B.C. The two most prominent of these areas were Syria (North), and Egypt (South). Syria was ruled by the Greek Seleucus and his descendants, while Egypt was ruled by the Greek Ptolemy and his line of descendants including the famous Cleopatra.

D. Daniel 11

Dan 11 is perhaps the most amazingly detailed historical prophecy to be found anywhere in the Bible. It continually speaks of the wars and relations between the king of the north (Seleucids), and the king of the south (Ptolemies) between the years 311 and 164 B.C. Such detailed predictions as these cause unbelieving critics to deny that Daniel could possibly be prophecy at all. The critics declare that Daniel must have been written about 165 B.C., *after* the events had occurred, because the details are too minute and accurate to be predictions. That claim flows out of the presupposition that there is no God--thus no such thing as predictive prophecy. But, if there is a God, then true prophecy leaps from the realm of impossibility to reality when given through a man connected with God.

IV. THE FOUR KINGDOMS AND HISTORY

Even as Daniel predicted, four distinct kingdoms succeeded each other in the period between the exile and the advent. Babylon, Medo-Persia, Greece, and Rome in turn exercised dominion over the Mediterranean and the near eastern world. Palestine is at the conjunction of the land masses that form the crossroads leading north and east to Asia, south to Africa, and westward toward Europe. It is strategic geographically, politically, militarily, and now for mineral resources as well. The ancient Children of Israel occupied that land as they awaited the coming of their Messiah, but they were mere pawns in the chess game that belonged to the larger nations.

A. Babylon

The Neo-Babylonian kingdom came to power when Nabopolassar, the father of Nebuchadnezzar, defeated the once great but decaying Assyrian empire. Nabopolassar rebelled from the Assyrians in 626 B.C. and continued to inch northward in further conquest year by year. Finally, having made a non-agression pact with the Medes, Nabopolassar and the Medes joined forces against the teetering Assyrians at their capital of Nineveh in 614 B.C. Nineveh fell two years later. The Assyrians were defeated at the Battle of Carchemish several years later. Pharaoh Necho II of Egypt sought to help Assyria but was too late. King Josiah of Judah was killed in a futile attempt to prevent Pharaoh from reaching Carchemish on the Euphrates River (2 Kings 23:29-30).

Nebuchadnezzar was in charge of his father's army, and took over the kingdom upon the death of Nabopolassar in about 605 B.C. The biblically significant highlights of his lengthy reign were his three invasions of Palestine in which he deported many of the people of Judah. Daniel was taken in the first deportation about 605 B.C. Other deportations took place in 597 and in 587 B.C. Ezekiel was taken away to Babylon, probably in 597 B.C., while Jeremiah wrote his *Book of Lamentations* over the destruction of Jerusalem and Solomon's temple in 586 B.C. In 571 B.C. Nebuchadnezzar took Tyre and controlled a large and prosperous territory while maintaining friendly relations on the east with the Medes.

When Nebuchadnezzar died in 562 B.C. he had accomplished a great deal. The Syriac or Aramaic language he used was the *lingua franca* or trade language for the world (Dan 2:4). Militarily he was a great warrior, leader, and conqueror who had forged an empire. Astrology and art were also advanced during his reign. He was also one of the last of the ancient absolute monarchs. His word meant either life or death (Dan 2:12-13).

After Nebuchadnezzar's death came a series of weaker rulers such as Nebuchadnezzar's son, Evil-Merodak (561-560), then Nebuchadnezzar's son-in-law, Nergalshareser (559-555). Nergalshareser's son, Labashi-Merodak (555), then ruled for one year before committing suicide amidst general rebellion and anarchy. Nabonidus came next (555-539), but he shared the throne with his biblically more famous son, Belshazzar (Dan 5:1-30; 7:1; 8:1).

What did the Jews learn during their Babylonian captivity (generally referred to as the *seventy year* period from 605-535 B.C.--Jer 25:11; 29:10; Dan 9:2)? The answer is several important things. They learned that (1) "the Most High rules in the kingdom of men and gives it to whomever He chooses" (Dan 4:32); (2) idols are powerless, but that "our God whom we serve is able to deliver us" (Dan 3:17); (3) God answers prayer (Dan 2:18-19) and keeps His promises to Israel (Dan 9:20-22); (4) the Messiah would come, but not for many hundreds of years (Dan 9:24-27); and (5) Israel would go through a time of trouble and persecution (Dan 8:9-12), but would survive with God's help (Dan 8:13-14, 25).

B. Medo-Persia

Astyages of Media (north of Babylon) and Cyrus II of Persia combined their efforts against Babylonia, and Cyrus later succeeded in overthrowing the decadent kingdom of Nabonidus and his son Belshazzar in 539 B.C. Actually, the Medes were subject to the Persians

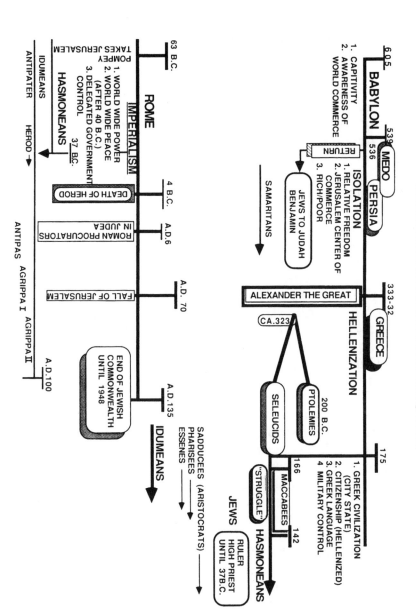

Time line for New Testament Background

under Cyrus' rule from 555 B.C., so they are considered a united kingdom.

In 536 B.C. Cyrus allowed 42,360 Jews to return to Israel headed by Zerubbabel (Ezra 2:1-2, 64). The Israelites reinstituted the overturned sacrificial system (Ezra 3:1-7) and began to work on rebuilding a temple (Ezra 5:1-2), since Nebuchadnezzar had destroyed the one Solomon constructed. The prophecies of Haggai and Zechariah occur during that rebuilding.

Cyrus II, who had been good to Israel as prophesied by Isaiah (44:28-45:13), was killed in battle in 529 B.C. He was succeeded by Cambyses II (529-522) who captured Egypt. Cambyses' brother Bardiya had a short reign before falling to the sword of Darius I. Darius ruled for about forty years and maintained five capitals: (1) Susa, the old Elamite capital in the south (Dan 8:2; Esth 1:2); (2) Ecbatana, the old Median capital; (3) Pasayadae, where Cyrus was buried; (4) Persepolis, where Darius ruled; and (5) Babylon.

Darius I extended the limits of Persian-held territory across Asia Minor (Anatolia), or present-day Turkey, to the Aegean Sea (Dan 8:4, 20). He came into Greece, but was defeated at the famous Battle of Marathon in 490 B.C. After appointing Xerxes as his successor and preparing to return in revenge to capture Athens, he died in 486 B.C. Darius left his mark, quite literally, on the side of a great 300 foot high cliff called the Behistun Stone, where his greatness was inscribed in three languages--Elamite, Persian, and Akkadian. It was not until the 19th century that the British soldier Henry Rawlinson copied and deciphered the languages, thus opening up thousands of tablets found in these languages.

Xerxes reigned next (486-464 B.C.) and was the biblical Ahasuerus who chose Esther the Jewess to be his queen. The hand of God's providence is seen quite remarkably in the Old Testament book bearing Esther's name. It shows that a sizeable portion of the Jewish population did not return to Palestine with Zerubbabel and thus became what is commonly termed the Diaspora, the Jews of the dispersion living outside of Israel among the Gentiles. Xerxes was more a lover than a man of war, and was defeated decisively at the Battle of Salamis in 480 B.C., and in several more battles the following year. He was killed in 464 B.C. in a harem intrigue.

Artaxerxes Longimanus followed Xerxes and was able to make peace with Greece and thus had a fairly long, peaceful and prosperous reign (464-424 B.C.). The events of Ezra who returned to Israel in 458 B.C., and those of Nehemiah who returned in 445 B.C., occurred during Artaxerxes' time. Herodotus (445 B.C.) also wrote his history (in Greek) during this period, and the Elaphantine Papyri in Egypt (much in Aramaic) show great similarities with language of the 5th century B.C. Ezra.

The rest of the Persian rulers down to the time of Alexander the Great are lesser known and ruled during the final years before the Persian overthrow by Greece. Darius II (424-404 B.C.) was followed by Artaxerxes II (404-358) who was succeeded by Artaxerxes III who was poisoned (358-338). Arses reigned two years (338-336) also being poisoned before Darius III (336-330) who was defeated totally by Alexander the Great. From 341 B.C. the Persians ruled a weakened Egypt as well, but were forced to surrender it all to Alexander within a decade.

An insight into the Medo-Persian law system is given in both Dan 6 and in Esther. Once a law was signed by the king (Esth 8:8), it could not be altered or revoked. Daniel accurately described it as "the law of the Medes and Persians, which does not alter" (Dan 6:8).

The setting of the ficticious Jewish story of Judith is during the Persian period. Some interesting insights--both about Persian culture and Jewish life--can be gleaned from those sixteen brief chapters.

C. Greece

Until the days of Philip of Macedon and his son Alexander the Great, Greece existed as a group of independent city states, perhaps loosely confederated at times. By force, Alexander conquered Thebes and Athens before he was even twenty years of age. The rest of Greece fell in behind him after that. He then led 5,000 horsemen and nearly 25,000 infantry into Asia Minor against the Persian king, Darius III. Darius retreated after an initial defeat in the west, and was soundly beaten at Issus in the east (333 B.C.). Alexander then turned south and captured Tyre, Damascus, Gaza, and all of Egypt. He was welcomed and crowned as Pharaoh in 331 B.C. Turning eastward he took each of the five Persian capitals and went as far as India. His life was cut short by illness and debauchery in 323 B.C. at the young age of 33.

Alexander's generals fought each other for possession of his territories and by 300 B.C. four distinct victors emerged. (1) Cassander held Greece and Macedonia. (2) Lysimachus controlled Thrace and the western part of Asia Minor, but later forfeited those territories to the Seleucids. (3) Seleucus I took northern Palestine and as much of Persia as he could control. (4) Ptolemy ruled over Egypt and southern Palestine. This division was predicted several times by Daniel. Dan 7:6 describes the Grecian kingdom as a leopard with *four* heads. In Dan 8, Greece is pictured as a male goat with one large horn. Verses 21b-22 say, "The large horn that is between its eyes is the first king [Alexander]. As for the broken horn and the four that stood up in its place, four kingdoms shall arise out of that nation, but not with its power."

The result of Alexander's conquests was what is called **Hellenization,** from the Greek word *hella,* which means Greece. To Hellenize is to Grecianize. Hellenization touched numerous areas of life including the following. (1) The Greek *language* was spread everywhere. (2) Greek literature, drama, sculpture, and art were circulated among the people. (3) The Greek city-state was established. The cities of the Decapolis in Palestine were part of this (Matt 4:25; Mark 5:20; 7:31). (4) The Greek architecture for buildings and construction prevailed with its ornate columns. (5) Greek culture and customs were adopted everywhere. This included Greek religion and gods, games, clothing styles, monetary systems, warfare tactics, and so forth. Greek became such a world-wide language that the New Testament was written in that very medium.

D. Rome

Although Rome may trace its founding to Romulus and Remus in 753 B.C., her increase in political power and her geographical spread over the Mediterranean region took place during the three Punic Wars with Carthage and the events that immediately followed (264-133 B.C.). Carthage, located just south of Rome on the North African coast, was a notable obstacle to Roman expansion. In fact, Rome was practically brought to her knees by Hannibal's elephants and 40,000 troops near Rome at the Battle of Cannae in 216 B.C. Consul Scipio Africanus, however, carried the battle to Carthage and defeated Hannibal completely at Zama in 202 B.C. Hannibal later made his way to Syria and joined Antiochus Epiphanes in his subjugation of the Jews (complete with elephants, 1 Macc 6:30, 34-37). The final crushing of Carthage came in the Third Punic War (149-146 B.C.), when Scipio Africanus minor leveled the city.

In 146 B.C. Rome also annexed Greece and Macedonia into the Roman Republic. When the King of Pergamum died in 133 B.C. he willed his territories to Rome. Rome consolidated her gains until in 65 B.C. only Mithradates VI of Asia Minor blocked Rome's vision of complete domination of the Mediterranean. Pompey, a Roman general, disposed of Mithradates in 64 B.C., and a year later entered Jerusalem to settle a dispute between two Hasmonean leaders, Hyrcanus and Aristobulus.

Pompey was a great leader and was married to the daughter of Julius Caesar, his rival. During the conquest of Egypt in 47 B.C. Pompey was murdered. Cleopatra and her brother, Ptolemy XII, ruled Egypt until Caesar came, married Cleopatra, and took her back to Rome with their new baby. Herod's father, Antipater II, helped Caesar conquer Egypt.

After Caesar's untimely death in 44 B.C., Anthony and Octavian were left as Rome's leaders. They were allied by Antony's marriage to Octavian's daughter. However, when Antony met Cleopatra in Damascus, he fell in love and returned with her to Egypt. Antony was later defeated in battle with Octavian at Actium in 31 B.C. A year later Antony and Cleopatra committed suicide, leaving Octavian the ruler of

ROMAN GOVERNMENT IN NEW TESTAMENT TIMES

EMPEROR ——————→ ROMAN ——— ROMAN SENATE

IMPERIAL PROVINCES	SENATORIAL PROVINCES

IMPERIAL PROVINCES

(12 in 27 B.C.)
(All frontier areas needing an army to hold the people in subjection)

LEGATE
(Called Prefects and Propraetors-- personally responsible to Caesar)

PROCURATORS
(Governors--usually over a sub-province such as Judea)

Cilicia--Gal 1:21, Acts 6:9
Galatia--Gal 1:2
Syria--Gal 1:21
Spain--Rom 15:24
Gaul--2 Tim 4:10
Illyrium--Rom 15:19,
(Dalmatia--2 Tim 4:10)

SENATORIAL PROVINCES

(10 in 27 B.C.)
(Peaceful Countries)

PROCONSULS
(Normally ex-praetors and ex-consuls)

QUAESTOR
(Received all revenues)

Cyprus--Acts 13:4, 7
Asia--Acts 19:10
Achaia--Acts 18:12
Macedonia--Acts 16:12

Pontus--1 Peter 1:1
Bithynia--Acts 16:7
Cappadocia--1 Peter 1:1
Pamphylia--Acts 13:13
Lycia--Acts 27:5

Judea became part of the Province of Syria in 63 B.C. Judea was a kingdom from 40 B.C. to A.D. 6, and again from A.D. 41-44 under Herod Agrippa I.

Egypt and of all Rome. In 27 B.C. Octavian was declared Emperor and took the title of Caesar Augustus. Luke 2:1 begins the Christmas story with, "And it came to pass in those days that a decree went out from Caesar Augustus that all the world should be registered."

Rome's contributions to the world were varied, but several should be mentioned. (1) The *Pax Romana* (Roman peace) resulted from her conquests and military might. Nations behaved under Rome's watchful eye during the entire reign of Augustus (27 B.C.-A.D. 14), and beyond. (2) The *legal system* of Rome for the most part was fair and just and improved upon that of the Greeks. Men learned to obey the law. (3) *Communication* and *transportation* were greatly improved, allowing travel to all parts of the empire. This allowed Christianity to spread rapidly. (4) Rome became a *world community* with peoples from all lands blending together their ideas and customs. This prepared people for a church that would incorporate all--every tongue, tribe, and ethnic group. (5) The Roman system of *government* was superior in many ways to those which preceded it. It was highly centralized and organized under the Emperor and the Senate. Each controlled about 14-16 provinces. The Imperial provinces were Syria, Galatia, Egypt, and other faraway places that might need military supervision. The Senatorial provinces, on the other hand, were Italy, Achaia, Sicily, and other relatively calm and near-at-hand areas.

V. THE MACCABEES AND HASMONEANS

It must be remembered that both the Seleucids who controlled Syria and the Ptolemies who controlled Egypt, were Greeks who imposed their wills upon the native populations. Palestine lay in between these two powerful dynasties and received its share of rough treatment. Both groups sought to control the Israelite territory. The Ptolemies succeeded in that desire in large measure from 300-198 B.C. Then Antiochus III, the Great, wrested control until his death in 175 B.C.

Antiochus IV, called Epiphanes, ruled from 175 to his death in about 164 B.C. Suffering a humiliation in Egypt by the Ptolemies who sought help from Rome, Antiochus Epiphanes began to vent his anger on Israel. He tried to impose worship of the Greek god Zeus upon the Jews, forbid the reading of the Old Testament and the keeping of the Sabbath, and outlawed circumcision. He desecrated the Jewish temple (2nd temple completed under Zerubbabel and Haggai) by setting up an altar to Zeus there and by offering a sow on that altar. This occurred in about 168/167 B.C.

The result was rebellion by many faithful Jews. Others, not so faithful, capitulated to the demands of Antiochus Epiphanes. The leaders of the Jewish rebellion were Mattathias and his sons Judas Maccabeus, Jonathan, and Simon. Against great odds (40,000 to 4,000 in some battles), the Jewish freedom fighters won significant clashes and by December 25, 165/64 B.C. they rid themselves of their Seleucid overlords, cleansed, and rededicated the temple in Jerusalem. Supposedly,the supply of oil for the lamp in the temple was to expire after only one day, but miraculously it continued burning for eight days until a fresh supply was obtained (1 Macc 4:52-59). That feast, commemorated every year since that day, was called the Feast of Dedication, or

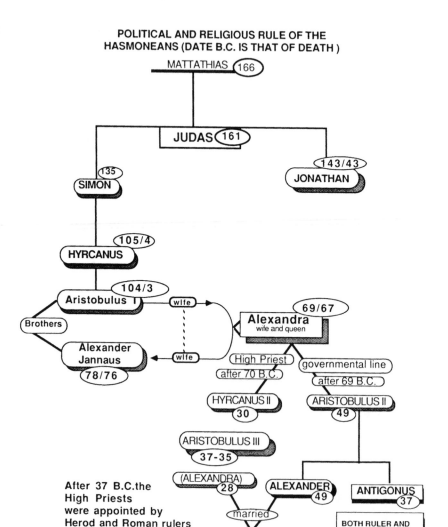

POLITICAL AND RELIGIOUS RULE OF THE
HASMONEANS (DATE B.C. IS THAT OF DEATH)

MATTATHIAS (166)

JUDAS (161)

JONATHAN (143/43)

SIMON (135)

HYRCANUS (105/4)

Aristobulus I (104/3) — wife →

Brothers

Alexander Jannaus (78/76) ← wife —

Alexandra (69/67) wife and queen

High Priest after 70 B.C. — HYRCANUS II (30)

governmental line after 69 B.C. — ARISTOBULUS II (49)

ARISTOBULUS III (37-35)

(ALEXANDRA) (28) — married — MARIAMNE I

ALEXANDER (49)

ANTIGONUS (37)

After 37 B.C. the High Priests were appointed by Herod and Roman rulers

BOTH RULER AND HIGH PRIEST from 40-37 B.C.

Hanukkah. Jesus attended it during His ministry, and John notes that it came in the winter (John 10:22). Hanukkah, therefore, celebrated by modern Jews near Christmas time, actually originated more than 160 years B.C.

Although Mattathias never lived to see the cleansing of the temple (he died in 166 B.C.), his son Judas led the effort until his death in battle in 161 B.C. Brother Jonathan ruled until his death in 143 B.C., and was succeeded by his brother Simon who lived until 135 B.C. The entire story is told from two viewpoints in 1 and 2 Macc in the Apocrypha (see chapter 6). The Jews even declared Simon their perpetual "prince, and high priest for ever, till there should arise a faithful prophet" (1 Macc 14:41, Douay). Simon passed his perpetual office on to his son John Hyrcanus (135-105 B.C.). From Hyrcanus onward, the family called itself the Hasmoneans. John was followed by his son Aristobulus (105-104), and then by John's other son, Alexander Jannaus (104-78). Both Aristobulus and Alexander Jannaus were married in succession to the same woman--Alexandra--who became the real power behind the throne. She continued to rule on her own for about ten years (78-69 B.C.), after the death of her second husband, Alexander Jannaus.

From that point, 70 or 69 B.C., the jobs of high priest, and that of governmental ruler were separated. Two of Alexandra's sons divided up those positions. Hyrcanus II became high priest, while Aristobulus II became ruler until 49 B.C. when his son Antigonus took over.

In 40 B.C. Herod the Great, an Idumean and a descendant of Esau, conquered the land. In order to give himself some legitimacy among the Jews, he married Mariamne I who was the granddaughter of the high priest Hyrcanus II, as well as the granddaughter of the ruler Aristobulus II, a true Hasmonean (see chapter 4 on Herod).

Part of the background that this Maccabean history provides is found in the fighting that occurred among the sects and parties who either supported or opposed the Hasmoneans. The high priesthood should not have been, biblically speaking, in the Hasmonean house, since they were not of Aaron's lineage. The Pharisees and Sadducees fought for power in some of these areas as well as over various doctrinal issues (see chapter 7).

VI.   THE SAMARITANS, IDUMEANS, AND NABATEANS

Three other peoples play a role on the pages of the New Testament--the Samaritans, Idumeans, and Nabateans. It is good to have a general idea of their background and development.

A.   The Samaritans

Jesus' parable of the good Samaritan (Luke 10:30-37), and His successful soul-winning effort with the Samaritan woman at the well of Sychar introduce New Testament readers to the Samaritans. Why was there a general coolness between Samaritans and Jews in Jesus' day?

When the capital city (Samaria) of the northern kingdom fell to Shalmaneser and the Assyrians in 722 B.C., many of the Israelites of the surrounding territory were relocated into far-off Assyrian towns. The Assyrians took the best craftsmen and artisans they could find from Samaria. But in return, they brought back to Samaria many people from their own land. 2 Kings 17:6, 18, 23 and 18:9-

POWER INFLUENCES IN PALESTINE
(100 B.C -- A.D.39)

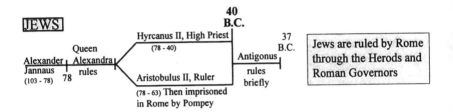

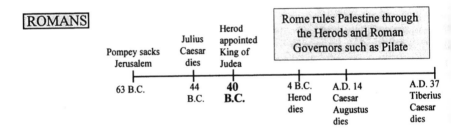

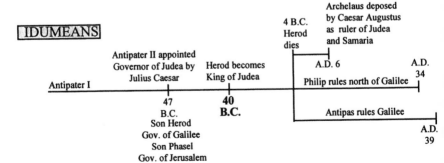

11 speak of the deportation of the Israelites. The relocation of foreigners into the Samaria region is related in 2 Kings 17:24, where they "placed them in the cities of Samaria instead of the children of Israel, and they took possession of Samaria and dwelt in its cities." They were not a pious sort of people as 2 Kings 17:25-34 indicates. Thus a people who were mixed racially as well as religiously were proliferated.

Added to this was the old antipathy between north and south in Israel. The Samaritans were not allowed to help rebuild the temple under Zerubbabel (Ezra 4:4-24; Neh 4:1-8). This general antipathy increased and intensified until in the time of Christ it had become practically a national policy on both sides.

B.   The Idumeans

The land of Idumea is mentioned four times in the Old Testament but only once in the New Testament (Mark 3:8) where it designates a region from which men and women followed Jesus. Idumea is the land south of Judea and was inhabited by the Edomites who moved into that region sometime after the fall of Jerusalem in 586 B.C. That movement was accelerated by the fall of Petra, the ancient capital of Edom, into the hands of the Nabateans in 300 B.C.

Judas Maccabeus recaptured Hebron from the Idumeans in 165 B.C. (1 Macc 4:29, 61; 5:65). John Hyrcanus further humiliated the Idumeans in 126 B.C. when he compelled them to be circumcised and to become practicing Jews. However, the tables were turned later. While the Hasmoneans were squabbling among themselves, Antipater II, the governor of Idumea, went to the aid of Julius Caesar in his campaign in Egypt in 46 B.C. In return, Caesar made Antipater procurator of Judea, Samaria, and Galilee. Five years later, Antipater's son, Herod the Great, was appointed King of the Jews by the Roman Senate. This brought to fulfillment a part of Isaac's blessing on Esau--"You shall break his yoke from your neck" (Gen 27:40). The irony of it all is that Herod, a descendant of *Esau,* was the king over the descendants of *Jacob.*

C. The Nabateans

The Nabateans were a nomadic people who became increasingly strong east of the Jordan with the decline of the Seleucid and Ptolemaic empires after 200 B.C. They captured and occupied Petra, and at one time controlled the territory as far north as Damascus. In the early Maccabean period they supported the Jews against the hellenization of the Seleucids, but later they fought against Alexander Jannaus (and won) in 85 B.C. Herod defeated the Nabateans in 31 B.C., but Herod Antipas was bested by Aretas IV. Antipas had divorced his wife, who was Aretas IV's daughter, to marry the wicked Herodias. The single biblical mention of the Nabateans is that of Damascus being under the control of Aretas IV when Paul escaped in a basket (2 Cor 11:32-33).

VII. FOR REVIEW AND DISCUSSION

1. What are the important geographical, political, historical, and racial connections the New Testament has with the Old Testament and/or the world of the first century B.C./A.D.?

2. Be able to identify the important Old Testament persons and events with their proper dates and vice versa.

3. Explain precisely how Dan 2 and 7 predict four successive world empires.

4. What significance do Dan 8 and 11 have historically? What nations and time periods do they each cover?

5. In outline fashion recount the basic history of the four kingdoms Daniel predicted.

6. How did each of these four kingdoms affect the Jews and/or prepare the way for Christianity?

7. Who were the Maccabees; what was their struggle; and how did their descendants set the stage for the New Testament world?

8. Precisely what is hellenization, and what effect did it have on the world?

9. What contributions did Rome make to the world?

10. Who were the Samaritans and why was there antipathy between them and the Jews in Christ's day?

11. How did the Idumeans fit into the first century B.C. history of Israel?

12. What is the historical background for the biblical reference to Aretas in 2 Cor 11:32?

VIII.   FOR FURTHER READING AND RESEARCH

Achtemeier, Paul J., Joel B. Green, and Marianne Meye Thompson. *Introducing the New Testament.* Grand Rapids: Eerdmans, 2001. xii + 624.

Burkett, Delbert Royce. *An Introduction to the New Testament and the Origins of Christianity.* Cambridge, UK: Cambridge University Press, 2002. xv + 600.

Cate, Robert L. *A History of the New Testament and Its Times*. Nashville: Broadman, 1991. 348 pp.

Drane, John William. *Introducing the New Testament*. Minneapolis: Fortress, 2001. 480 pp.

Ehrlich, Ernst Ludwig. *A Concise History of Israel from the Earliest Times to the Destruction of the Temple in A.D. 70*. New York: Harper & Row, 1965. vi + 153.

Fairweather, William. *The Background of the Gospels*. Edinburgh: T. & T. Clark, 1926. xxiv + 456.

_____. *From the Exile to the Advent*. 5th ed. Edinburgh: T. & T. Clark, 1952. 210 pp.

Foerster, Werner. *From the Exile to Christ*. Trans. Gordon E. Harris. Philadelphia: Fortress, 1964. xiv + 247.

Gromacki, Robert Glenn. *New Testament Survey*. Grand Rapids: Baker Book House, 1987. pp. 1-39.

Leschert, Dale F. *The Flow of the New Testament*. Fearn: Mentor, 2002. 524 pp.

Moss, R. Wadi. *From Malachi to Matthew*. London: Charles H. Kelly, 1893. xvi + 256.

Niswonger, Richard L. *New Testament History*. Grand Rapids: Zondervan, 1988. 332 pp.

Rupprecht, Arthur A. "The Cultural and Political Setting of the New Testament." *The Expositor's Bible Commentary: Introductory Articles*. Ed. Frank Gaebelein. Grand Rapids: Zondervan, 1979. I, 483-498.

Russell, David Syme. *Between the Testaments*. Philadelphia: Fortress, 1968. 176 pp.

Tenney, Merrill Chapin, and Walter M. Dunnett. *New Testament Survey*. Grand Rapids: Eerdmans, 1985. xix + 454.

Witherington, Ben. *New Testament History A Narrative Account*. Grand Rapids: Baker , 2001. 430 pp.

_____. *The New Testament Story*. Grand Rapids: Eerdmans, 2004. x + 283.

3

UNDERSTANDING PALESTINE'S PHYSICAL GEOGRAPHY

The importance of understanding Palestine's physical geography cannot be overemphasized for the student of the New Testament. Pastors and teachers of the Word are at a definite disadvantage if their congregation has been to "the Holy Land" (Zech 2:12), and they have not. The best course this writer ever took in the geography of Israel was a thirty day intensive study tour of Israel and the near east. I have since been a teaching instructor on numerous additional Holy Land tours.

I. THE FOUR NATURAL REGIONS

From the accompanying map of Palestine's physical features, one can readily see that there are four natural regions that run north-south through the land. These four regions--coast, hills, rift, and trans-Jordan--will be explained in that order, that is, from west to east.

A. The Coast

Along the Mediterranean Sea is a fairly level coastal region that is only a few miles wide at some points and up to 25 miles wide in other areas, especially farther south. In ancient times the Phoenicians and Philistines controlled these flat coastal plains.

Several things should be noted about the coastal region. (1) It was a wonderful passage way for armies moving through the region. In fact, it was referred to as the *Via Maris* or Way of the Sea. (2) The Carmel Mountain Range, running nearly 2,000 feet high, completely blocks the coastal area clear to the ocean. (3) Three narrow passes (heavy dark lines on map) dissect the Carmel Range, allowing north-south travel. From west to east these passes are: (a) Yokneam; (b) Megiddo; and (c) Dothan. It will be remembered that Jacob's son, Joseph, was sold at Dothan to a caravan heading down into Egypt (Gen 37:17, 25). The caravan may have taken the Dothan Pass through the Carmel Range and then followed the *Via Maris* down the coast.

(4) A Fourth feature of the coastal region is the *shephelah*--an area of low-lying hills that connect the coast with the higher hills region. The hills region is so steep on both the west and the east, that the access to the hills area is extremely limited. The Shephelah allows passage into the larger hills. For this reason, it was a strategic area and was closely guarded by fortified cities in ancient times, *e.g.* Gath, Eglon, Libnah, Lachish, Tel Beit Mirsim. (5) There is no natural source of fresh water in the coastal region (except rain). No rivers run there. Only water from cisterns or wells was available in ancient times (Gen 21:14-15, 21, 25; 26:18). When Herod the Great built Caesarea on the coast, he constructed an aqueduct that

stretched for twelve miles northward to
Carmel.   (6) The coastal region is very fertile and
receives ample rainfall. It is choice agricultural
land--flat, fertile, and free of so many rocks that
generally cover Israel's terrain.

B. The Hills

The hills region   also   runs north and south.
The elevation in upper Galilee reaches 3,800 feet,
and 2,500-3,000 is maintained for most of its
course southward until it begins to taper off and
level out around Beersheba. Access into the hills
region is difficult and very limited, especially on
the eastern side where the mountains drop off
precipitiously in some places for several thousand
feet.

Some interesting features of the hills region
are: (1) The Jezreel Valley cuts completely
through the hills, allowing east-west traffic to
pass easily through this fertile valley. The Battle
of Armageddon will be fought in this valley that is
on the average 10-15 miles wide and 30 miles long.
The three passes through the Carmel Range
connect the Jezreel Valley with the coastal
region.   (2) The agriculture of the hills region is
far from ideal--mainly allowing olive, fig, and
grape production and a few patches of grain in
quite rocky fields. It is good, however, for
shepherding sheep. David's home at Bethlehem
was in the hill region.   (3) Some key biblical cities
were situated in the hill region--Hebron, Shiloh,
Gibeah, Bethel, Jerusalem, Samaria, Shechem,
Cana, and Nazareth which overlooks the north
side of the Jezreel Valley. Of Nazareth Luke
records, "and they led Him to the brow of the hill
on which their city was built, that they might
throw Him down over the cliff," (Luke 4:29).

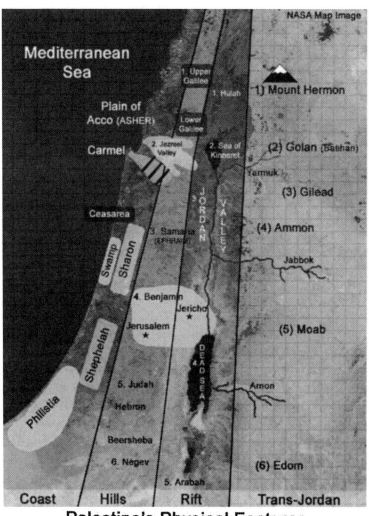

Palestine's Physical Features

C.   The Rift

The largest and longest geological fault in the world runs from Lebanon down through Israel, under the Red Sea and clear into the horn of eastern Africa. In Israel the land on either side of the rift, an enormously deep valley, is about 3,000-4,000 feet higher than the rift itself. The rift valley is about 10 miles wide and possesses Israel's only river, the Jordan.

Some interesting facts about the rift region are: (1) The rift contains Israel's largest sources of fresh water, the Jordan River and the Sea of Galilee, a lake 8 miles wide and 13 miles long. Today that water is pumped to Israel's cities and agricultural stations.   (2) The Sea of Galilee is 700 feet below sea level, more than twice the negative elevation of Death Valley, the lowest point in the United States. Consequently, the climate is warm and tropical, and tourists are surprised to see large fields of bananas being cultivated. (3) The primary biblical cities of the rift were Hazor (Josh 11:1; Judg 4:2), Jericho, Sodom and Gomorrah, Capernaum, Caesarea Philippi, and Tiberias (John 6:1). The latter city was built between A.D. 17-22 by Herod Antipas in honor of Tiberias Caesar (Luke 3:1).   (4) The Dead Sea is the lowest point on earth, about 1,300 feet *below* sea level. The only road through the Dead Sea area is on its western side. The cliffs on the east side come right down to the water.   (5) The rift is quite fertile for the most part, though irrigation is required in the southern reaches where rainfall is limited to about one inch per year!

D.   The Trans-Jordan

The term trans-Jordan means *across* the Jordan. It is the area on the eastern side of the

Jordan River. In general, it is 3,000-4,000 feet in elevation and is considerably drier than the coastal and hill regions to the west.

As the accompanying map indicates, the trans-Jordan region divides naturally into six parts, separated by the Yarmuk, Jabbok, and Arnon Rivers. Each of these rivers is more like a dry stream bed, or wadi, most of the year. Nevertheless, in ancient times they marked off the regions where different peoples lived.

Mount Hermon is the tallest mountain in all of Palestine, rising to an elevation of 9,232 feet. Its melting snows feed the headwaters of the Jordan River, and those of rivers flowing into Syria and Lebanon. It may have been on one of its lower peaks that Jesus was transfigured (Matt 16:13; 17:1-9).

Golan, Gilead, Ammon, Moab, and Edom are fairly dry plateau lands similar to the leeward side of many mountains. Moab and Edom to its south, are considerably drier than those lands to the north of them. In New Testament times the trans-Jordan fell into several administrative districts--Gaulanitis, Decapolis, and Perea. The major cities were Abila (Abilene, Luke 3:1), Gerasa, Philadelphia (ancient Rabbah and modern Amman, Jordan's capital), and Medeba.

II. THE CLIMATE OF PALESTINE

Climatologists classify Israel's climate as Mediterranean. From the northern border of Israel to Gaza in the south is roughly from 33° to 31° 30′ N. in latitude. The climate is almost identical to that of the coast of California from San Diego to Ensenada, Mexico, which is also classified as Mediterranean climate.

Rainfall comes in slowly moving storms each lasting 2-4 days, between November and March or April. The Old Testament referred to "the latter and former rain to the earth" (Hos 6:3), and James, in extolling the virtue of patience, says to note the farmer who waits "patiently for it [fruit] until it receives the early and latter rain" James 5:7). The initial rains in November come after a deadening six month drought. The hills spring forth in green (for the sheep), and the grain crops begin to germinate. The first ripe grains were brought in during March or April for the Feast of Firstfruits connected with the Passover celebration (Lev 23:4-14). The rest of the grain was harvested later in May in time for Pentecost (50 days after Passover, Lev 23:15-22). The calendar for harvesting grapes, figs, olives, fruits, and nuts was in our September or October just prior to the Feast of Tabernacles (Lev 23:33-44).

It is important to know that the rainfall is greatest along the coast (west), and in the north. The western side of the hills region also picks up plenty of rain, but the eastern slopes and rift get very little (2-4 inches tapering off the farther east one goes). Then the higher trans-Jordan hills again pick up the clouds and catch some precipitation but in diminished amounts. The rule of thumb is: *the points farther west and north get the most rain, while areas farther east and south get appreciably less rainfall.* The most notable exception to this rule is the Jezreel Valley. The clouds travel through the entire valley and bring rain through that corridor to the rich area just south of the Sea of Galilee.

Heat and cold vary in Palestine. It can easily be 85° swimming weather in January at the Dead Sea (southeast) and cold and windy on Mt. Carmel (northwest). Winter rarely brings freezing temperatures to the coast, and onshore breezes keep the coastal temperatures moderate even in summer. The summer heat elsewhere can be extreme, similar to the California and Arizona deserts. The hills region, however, receives ocean breezes somewhat due to its close proximity to the shore.

III. REQUIREMENTS FOR SETTLEMENTS

Four ingredients were necessary in ancient times for settlements to begin in Palestine. These requirements dictated where cities would arise. Without each of these elements a town could easily fail.

A. Water

A major necessity was a reliable water supply. Rainfall (only six months a year) could not supply this need adequately. Therefore, a natural spring or a well was needed. Jacob's well at Sychar is about 125 feet deep (John 4:11). The virgin's spring (Gihon) is Jerusalem's only perennial natural source of water. Megiddo was sustained by a well reached by deep stairs and eventually through a 100 foot tunnel. A dry season could spell disaster for that city's water resource.

B. Soil

A second ingredient needed for community was an area of usable soil. Grains and breads were the staff of life, and even hill country towns had to be near at least some fertile patches of ground. Agriculture was very important in ancient times, and contrary to modern farming methods, one farmer could not produce enough for hundreds of others.

C. Communication

A city also needed to be on a main road for easy travel, trade, and communication. There is one primary road from north to south in the hill region. Most of the major cities were on this thoroughfare--Shechem (near modern Nablus), Jerusalem, Bethlehem, Hebron, and Beersheba. Jericho, Capernaum, Tiberias, and Nazareth were all on primary highways.

D. Defense

There was also a strategic necessity--that of defense. A city needed to be able to defend some road or pass through an important area. The towns of the Shephelah defended access into the hill region. Yokneam, Megiddo, and Dothan guarded the northern entrances to the passes that bear their names. The important hill cities on the main road protected that road. Jericho was situated to close off both east-west and north-south travel. Matthew sat at the tax office in Capernaum because all those coming into Israel from the north and east would pass through that city (Matt 9:9).

IV. DISTANCES IN PALESTINE

The area of Palestine is relatively small when compared even with most of the States in the United States. I once asked a missionary to Israel what State he compared Israel to in size when he showed slides to an American audience. His reply was Connecticut--not one of the larger States by far. It is only 65 miles as the crow flies from the Sea of Galilee to the Dead Sea, and likewise only 70 miles from Nazareth to Bethlehem. Even the proverbial distance from Dan to Beersheba (1 Sam 3:20), measures only 148 miles. A mere 40 miles separate Jerusalem and Amman--the capitals of Israel and Jordan. Damascus, Syria's capital, is no more than 40 miles from Israel's northernmost settlements. The distance from Capernaum to Tyre (Mark 7:24) is less than 35 miles.

On a return trip from the Holy Land we took off from Amman, Jordan, and flew north until we came to Mt. Hermon, in just several minutes time. We then banked to the left, and I took a lovely picture of the view. The picture included Mt. Hermon in the foreground, then the nearby Sea of Galilee just beyond it, and in the background the Israeli coast on the Mediterranean Sea. The land is compact and distances are diminished.

One morning we left our hotel in Jerusalem and traveled by bus to visit the Galilee region in the north, returning again that evening. But, in Jesus' day, all of the many trips were on foot. Plus, Jesus had only about 1,300 days of public ministry. Half of those days were in the fall and winter (whether cold or rainy), and the other half fell in the much warmer spring and summer months. During all types of weather, Jesus traveled extensively by foot (Mark 1:38; Luke 10:1; John 4:40). It is hard to imagine a more strenuous and gruelling schedule that certainly demanded vigorous physical effort.

V.   FOR REVIEW AND DISCUSSION

1. Be able to name the four natural regions of Palestine in order from west to east, and list the important features of each area.

2. Discuss the climate of Palestine in relation to rainfall, temperature, and growing seasons.

3. What are the necessary ingredients for founding a city in Palestine? Discuss the importance of each point.

4. Did the concept of the nearness and close proximity of so many seemingly distant places in Israel surprise you? How did your view of the distances in Israel change? Do you see Christ and the Apostles in any different light as a result?

VI.   FOR FURTHER READING AND RESEARCH

Aharoni, Yohanan. *The Land of the Bible: A Historical Geography.* Trans. A. F. Rainey. Philadelphia: Westminster, 1967. xiv + 409.

Aharoni, Yohanan, and Yohanan Aharoni. *The Carta Bible Atlas.* Jerusalem: Carta, 2002. 223 pp.

Baly, Denis. *The Geography of the Bible.* New York: Harper & Row, 1974. xv + 288.

Beitzel, Barry J. *The Moody Atlas of Bible Lands.* Chicago: Moody, 1985. xx + 234.

Bimson, John J. Ed. *Baker Encyclopedia of Bible Places.* Grand Rapids: Baker, 1995. 319 pp.

Bimson, John J., and J. P. Kane. *New Bible Atlas.* Leicester England: Inter-Varsity Press, 1985. 128 pp.

Brisco, Thomas V. *Holman Bible Atlas.* Nashville: Broadman & Holman, 1998. xiv + 298.

Cleave, Richard L.W. *The Holy Land Satellite Atlas.* Vol 1. Terrain Recognition, Nicosia, Cyprus: Rohr Productions, 1999. 152 pp.

_____. *The Holy Land Satellite Atlas.* Vol. 2 The Regions. Nicosia, Cyprus: Rohr Productions, 2002. 248 pp.

Frank, Harry Thomas, ed. *Hammond's Atlas of the Bible Lands.* Maplewood, NJ: Hammond, 1977. 48 pp.

Kraeling, Emil G., ed. *Rand McNally Historical Atlas of the Holy Land.* New York: Rand McNally, 1959. 88 pp.

May, Herbert G., ed. *Oxford Bible Atlas.* London: Oxford University, 1962. 144 pp.

Pfeiffer, Charles F. *Baker's Bible Atlas.* Grand Rapids: Baker, 1965. 333 pp.

Pfeiffer, Charles F. and Howard F. Vos. *The Wycliffe Historical Geography of Bible Lands.* Chicago: Moody, 1967. xx + 604.

Wood, D. R. W., *et. al. New Bible Atlas.* Inter-Varsity, 1985. 128 pp.

Wright, George Ernest and Floyd Vivian Filson. *The Westminster Historical Atlas to the Bible.* Philadelphia: Westminster, 1945. 114 pp.

4

HEROD THE GREAT AND HIS DESCENDANTS

I. HEROD THE GREAT

Humanly speaking, Herod the Great may have been the most towering personage of his entire age--anywhere on earth. The conquests he made, the buildings he constructed, the power he wielded, the dynasty he left, and the fame still attached to his name all attest to the truth of that proposition.

A. The Life of Herod the Great

Herod was born in Idumea (Southern Palestine) in 73 B.C. during the reign of Queen Alexandra. His father, Antipater II, and his grandfather, Antipater I, were Idumeans by race and Jews by religion. Herod's mother, Kufra or Cypros, was the daughter of Hareth, King of Nabatea, an Arab. Herod had three brothers, Phasael, Joseph, and Pheroras, as well as a sister, Salome. As a youth, Herod associated with world travelers on occasion at Petra and gained a knowledge of their customs and languages. He was a good horseman and wrestler.

Herod's father, Antipater II, was appointed ruler of Judea and given the title of Procurator by Julius Caesar because he had helped Caesar and Cleopatra take over Egypt. At age 26 Herod was made governor of Galilee, then had Samaria and Coele-Syria placed under his rule. Within five years he had complete control over all of Palestine, but the Jews resented him, favoring instead the Hasmonean line.

Herod decided to use marriage to gain acceptance by the Jews. He became engaged to Mariamne, the granddaughter both of Hyrcanus II (the high priest), and of Aristobulus (the chief Hasmonean ruler). However, he would need to conquer militarily before he could rule as he wished. He was driven out of Jerusalem by Antigonus and the Parthians, barely escaping before gaining a victory in battle near Bethlehem.

He then went to Rome to gain further political backing for his ambitions in Palestine. Antony and Octavian aided him and he was appointed King of the Jews by the Roman Senate in 40 B.C., at age 33. Three years later he conquered Jerusalem after a five-month siege, defeating the forces of Antigonus, the Hasmonean ruler.

To gain control of the Jewish Sanhedrin, Herod killed 45 of the 71 member body and appointed his own loyalists instead. In Christ's day there was a party called the Herodians--those who felt it was best to go along with the policies of Herod, or Rome, or whoever else was in charge (Matt 22:16; Mark 3:6). He appointed an obscure priest named Ananel as High Priest, even though Mariamne and her mother Alexandra begged to have Mariamne's brother Aristobulus placed in the office. Herod later gave in, but about a year later Aristobulus "accidentally" drowned in Herod's swimming pool in Jericho.

Herod had received help from Mark Antony and named his newly constructed Jerusalem fortress the Antonia, after Mark Antony. However, when Antony and Cleopatra tried to build an eastern empire in Egypt, Octavian met and defeated Antony at the Battle of Actium in 31 B.C. Herod immediately traveled to Rhodes to meet with the sole head of the Roman empire, Octavian (age 32). Herod boldly pledged that even as he had been loyal to Antony, so he would be loyal to Octavian. Octavian took the title Caesar Augustus and ruled from 31 B.C. to A.D. 14 (Luke 2:1).

The following year, Herod's sister, Salome, falsely accused Mariamne of being unfaithful, and Herod had Mariamne put to death. He later regretted that unjust decision and mourned for her the rest of his life.

Herod's policy was to please both the Romans and the Jews. He became successful at both. He promoted the honor and welfare of Judaism (at home and abroad), while suppressing their yearning for nationalism. At the same time he honored Rome and sought to make Jerusalem the showcase city of the Roman empire. In accomplishing that latter goal, Herod financed enormous building projects. He eventually died at Jericho in March of 4 B.C. age 69.

B. The Legacy of Herod the Great

Herod the Great left enormous power and influence to his family and a series of buildings-- some of which remain intact to this very day. Evidences of Herodian construction are to be found throughout Israel.

Herod constructed a number of fortresses primarily to protect his family and himself from internal strife. **(1)** In Jerusalem the enormous *Antonia* towered above the temple area. Jesus was brought before Pilate on the Gabbatha or pavement of the Antonia (John 19:13), and Paul was taken up into the "castle" (*KJV*, Acts 21:34, 37; 22:24; 23:10), or Antonia fortress. **(2)** A second fortress and palace was built on a hill southeast of Bethlehem which he named the *Herodium*. It looks like a volcano from a distance. **(3)** Herod fortified the *Masada* on the west side of the Dead Sea, where eventually the Jewish zealots escaped from the Romans from A.D. 70-73. **(4)** John the Baptist was beheaded by Herod's son Antipas at *Macherias,* another fortress-palace, in the hills on the east side of the Dead Sea. **(5)** *Threx* and *Tauros* were built on either side of the Wadi Qilt above Jericho, and **(6)** *Docus* stood high above Jericho on the Mount of Temptation. **(7)** The *Alexandrium* east of Nablus on Mount Sartaba guarded access into Samaria as well as up and down the Jordan Valley. Each of these fortresses could signal one or two of the others. I have stood on the Herodium on a clear day and could see distinctly the location of the Antonia to the north as well as Macherias across the Dead Sea.

Herod also constructed a hippodrome for chariot racing in Jerusalem (guess where Ben Hur won the race), musical theatres, athletic amphitheatres, and many other cultural buildings. The city of Caesarea on the Mediterranean was Herod's project, including its huge viaduct and breakwater for a harbor. He brought water into Jerusalem from Bethlehem by means of a large stone pipe system, the remains of which can be seen in places today. His palace in Jerusalem, now the police headquarters, was a marvel in its day as well.

But Herod's greatest legacy was his reconstruction and beautification of the Temple, a project begun in 20 B.C. and still not completed 30 years after his death when Jesus entered the Temple. When Jesus said, "Destroy this Temple and in three days I will raise it up" (John 2:19), referring to His body, the Jews replied, "It has taken forty-six years to build this temple" (John 2:20), referring to Herod's Temple. It was enormously large, beautiful, and costly (Matt 24:1; Acts 3:1, 11). The Romans destroyed this temple when they captured Jerusalem in A.D. 70. Today, the Islamic Dome of the Rock is situated approximately where Herod's Temple stood. The Western Wall, sometimes called the Wailing Wall, was a retaining wall Herod built to enlarge the Temple area. It was about 200 feet high. The walls of Old Jerusalem itself were constructed by Herod as well. It seems that his projects were endless.

II. THE DESCENDANTS OF HEROD

Before Herod married Mariamne he had a wife named Doris. He later married a second Mariamne, a Samaritan named Malthace, a Cleopatra, and five others (ten in all). Herod had about fifteen children. Please refer to the chart on the Herodian dynasty when considering Herod's descendants.

A. Herod's Children

1. *Antipater*. The eldest son was Antipater, the child of Doris, Herod's first wife. Through intrigue with Herod's brother, Antipater falsely accused the two sons of Mariamne I of plotting

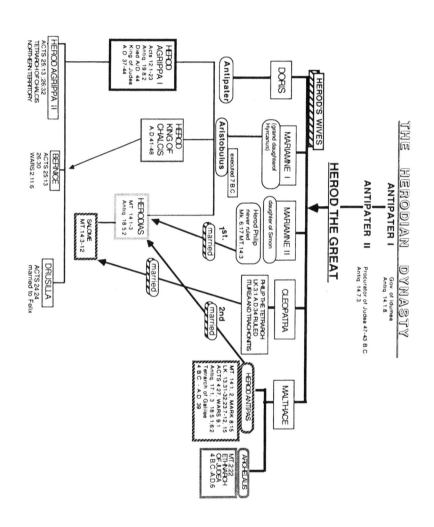

against Herod's life. Herod had them tried by a Roman court in Lebanon, then executed by strangling in Sebaste (Samaria) in 7 B.C. That action left Antipater as the heir to Herod's vast empire, until he also was caught plotting his father's death. He was put in chains until Rome gave Herod permission to kill him.

2. *Alexander and Aristobulus.* Mariamne I had three sons (one died young) and two daughters (Salampsio and Cyprus) before Herod had her killed. Her two living sons, Alexander and Aristobulus, were Herod's favorites, and would have succeeded him on the throne except for the treachery of Antipater (above) and Salome, Herod's sister. Salome wanted her own son to rule. Alexander and Aristobulus were both married and the young children of Aristobulus were brought up at Rome.

3. *Philip the Tetrarch.* Mentioned in Luke 3:1, Philip the Tetrarch was the son of Cleopatra (Jewish), Herod's fifth wife. He ruled Batanea, Trachonitis, Gaulanitis, Auranitis, and some areas around Jamnia. He ruled justly and built Caesarea Philippi at Paneas (Matt 16:13). He was married to Salome, the daughter of his brother Philip (and Herodias). Salome was the girl who danced for the head of John the Baptist (Matt 14:1-11). They had no children and so Philip's kingdom went back into Roman hands at his death in A.D. 34.

4. *Herod Philip.* Herod's second Mariamne was the daughter of the Jewish high priest Simon. She had one son, Herod Philip, who never ruled, but lived as a private citizen. He married Herodias, and they had a daughter, Salome (mentioned above), before Herodias divorced him (Matt 14:3; Mark 6:17).

5. ***Archelaus.*** Malthace, Herod's Samaritan wife, had two sons, Archelaus and Antipas. Both ruled. Archelaus was proclaimed king after his father's death and ruled from 4 B.C.-A.D. 6 over Judea, Idumea, Samaria, Caesarea, Sebaste, Joppa, and Jerusalem (Matt 2:2). He became wealthy, but was cruel and unjust. When he was accused of cruelty by the Jews, Caesar Augustus presided over his trial, and he was banished to Gaul in A.D. 7. Roman governors (including Pilate) then ruled over Judea. Joseph, who had fled to Egypt with Mary and Jesus, feared to return to *Judea* after Herod's death, because he heard that wicked Archelaus had taken over (Matt 2:22).

6. ***Antipas.*** Herod Antipas, the other son of Malthace, became ruler over Galilee and Perea. He was married to the daughter of Aretas IV, King of Nabatea, but divorced her to marry the wicked Herodias, the wife of his half-brother Philip (#4 above). Aretas IV then invaded Antipas' territory and demolished Antipas' entire army. This was the Herod who had John the Baptist beheaded (Matt 14:3-11; Luke 9:7-9), and who mocked Jesus in Jerusalem on the eve of Christ's crucifixion (Luke 23:6-12). Eventually, Antipas sought more power from Emperor Caligula but was banished to Gaul in A.D. 39 when Agrippa I falsely accused him of being in league with the Parthians.

B. Herod's Grandchildren

Mariamne I's son Aristobulus had three young children before Herod the Great killed him in 7 B.C. The children escaped death, were brought up in Rome, and knew all the people at the royal court.

1. ***Herod Agrippa I.*** Agrippa I lived in Rome, then under his uncle Antipas' care for a while, but with little success until he met and became friends with Caligula. For six months he was imprisoned in Rome for not binding his tongue in a remark about Tiberius Caesar. He was released in A.D. 37 after Tiberius' death, and Caligula, the new Emperor, gave Agrippa I the territories formerly ruled by Philip (A.3 above) and Lysanias. He also was given the title of King (Acts 12:1). In A.D. 39, he accused Antipas before Caligula and received all his territories. Later Emperor Claudius gave him Judea and Samaria as well. At that point his kingdom equalled that of Herod the Great in extent. The Jews loved him because he abided closely by the Law and tried to please them (by killing James and nearly Peter also, Acts 12:1-19). He died suddenly in A.D. 44, at age 54 (Acts 12:20-23; *Antiq.* xix.8.2), leaving three daughters and a son, Agrippa II, who was 17 years of age.

2. ***Herod, King of Chalcis.*** Agrippa I's brother, Herod, was the King of Chalcis, a city in the Bekah Valley in Lebanon, ancient Coele-Syria. He ruled until his death in A.D. 48 and was married to his niece, Bernice, the daughter of Agrippa I.

3. ***Herodias.*** Herodias was the daughter of Aristobulus and the sister of #1 and #2 just above. She was married first to her uncle Philip (A.4 above), and later to her uncle Antipas (A.6 above). She was wicked and ambitious and caused the downfall of Antipas when she urged him to ask Caligula for the title of king. She followed Antipas into banishment. It was she who urged her daughter Salome to ask for the head of John the Baptist because John had preached against her

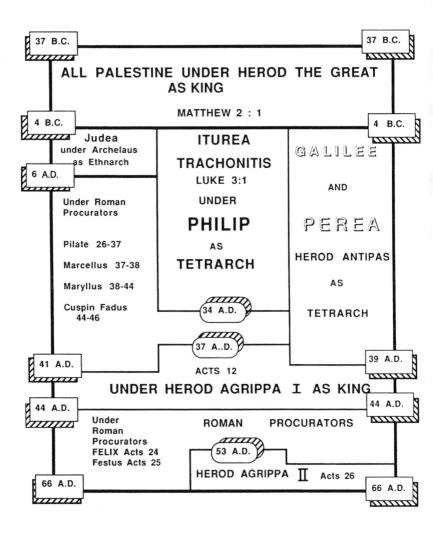

Palestine from the Accession of Herod to the Beginning
of the Judeo Roman War

37 B.C.

37 B.C.

ALL PALESTINE UNDER HEROD THE GREAT AS KING

MATTHEW 2 : 1

4 B.C.

4 B.C.

Judea
under Archelaus
as Ethnarch

ITUREA

TRACHONITIS

GALILEE

6 A.D.

LUKE 3:1

UNDER

AND

Under Roman
Procurators

PHILIP

PEREA

AS

Pilate 26-37

Marcellus 37-38

TETRARCH

HEROD ANTIPAS

Maryllus 38-44

AS

Cuspin Fadus
44-46

34 A.D.

TETRARCH

37 A..D.

41 A.D.

ACTS 12

39 A.D.

UNDER HEROD AGRIPPA I AS KING

44 A.D.

44 A.D.

Under
Roman
Procurators
FELIX Acts 24
Festus Acts 25

ROMAN   PROCURATORS

53 A.D.

HEROD AGRIPPA II   Acts 26

66 A.D.

66 A.D.

divorce and remarriage (Matt 14:3-11; *Antiq.* xviii.5.2).

C. Herod's Great-Grandchildren

Three children of Herod's grandson, Agrippa I, are mentioned in the New Testament along with Salome (already amply covered). Each of these three are found in Acts and each shared nobility, even though two were women.

1. *Herod Agrippa II.* Born in A.D. 27, young Agrippa II was only 17 when his father Agrippa I was eaten of worms and died in A.D. 44. But six years later, in A.D. 50, Emperor Claudius gave Agrippa II the lands of his uncle Herod, King of Chalcis, and two years later the territories of Philip and Lysanias along with the title of King. Agrippa I had been instrumental in bringing Claudius to power in Rome after the death of Caligula, so Claudius aided the young Agrippa II out of that friendship. Later Nero increased his domains. This same King Agrippa II heard the Apostle Paul in Caesarea and said,"You almost persuade me to become a Christian" (Acts 26:28; cf. 25:13). In A.D. 70 he fought with Rome against the Jews then retired to Rome and died in A.D. 100, the last ruling descendant of Herod the Great.

2. *Bernice.* As mentioned above, Bernice, daughter of Agrippa I, was married to Herod, King of Chalcis, in Lebanon (B.2). After his death in A.D. 48 she lived and traveled with her brother Agrippa II (Acts 25:13; 26:30), and raised suspicions in Rome of incest (*Wars* ii.11.6).

3. *Drusilla.* Drusilla, the sister of Agrippa II and Bernice, was married to the Roman Governor of Judea, Felix (Acts 24:24). Felix sought bribes and when he was replaced in office he left Paul

imprisoned in Caesarea as a favor to the Jews (Acts 24:24-27).

A colleague of mine told me that he once heard a preacher speak on Herod. He apparently had used a concordance to find all forty-four New Testament references to Herod. Unfortunately, only nine of those citations concerned Herod the Great. The poor preacher had confused and combined *four generations* of Herods into one giant message! Hopefully, the information recounted in this chapter will keep current readers from making the same blunder.

III. FOR REVIEW AND DISCUSSION

1. Briefly outline the major events and achievements of Herod the Great.
2. After studying the chart of the Herodian dynasty, try to reconstruct it as accurately as possible.
3. Which of the Herods are actually mentioned in the New Testament? Which ones played a major role? How?
4. Be able to associate the names of the territories which the major Herods ruled with their locations on a map.

IV. FOR FURTHER READING AND RESEARCH

Grant, Michael. *Herod the Great.* New York: American Heritage Press, 1971. 272 pp.

Hoehner, Harold W. "Herod." *International Standard Bible Encyclopedia.* Ed. G. W. Bromiley. Grand Rapids: Eerdmans, 1979. III, 688-698.

_____. "Herod." *The Zondervan Pictorial Encyclopedia of the Bible.* Ed. M. C. Tenney. Grand Rapids: Zondervan, 1975. III, 126-146.

_____. *Herod Antipas.* Cambridge [Eng.]: University Press, 1972. xvi + 436.

Josephus. *Antiquities.* xiv.1.3; 7:3; xiv.9-14; xvii.1.3; 2:2; xviii.5.1-4; 6:1-4; xix.7.3; 8.2; xx.7.7; *Wars.* 1.10-14; 1.28; 11.16; iv.1.3; 4.4.

Levine, Lee I. "Herod the Great." *The Anchor Bible Dictionary.* Ed. David Noel Freedman. New York: Doubleday, 1992. III, 161-169.

Perowne, Stewart. *The Later Herods: The Political Background of the New Testament.* New York: Abingdon Press, 1958. 216 pp.

_____. *The Life and Times of Herod the Great.* New York: Abingdon Press, 1959. 216 pp.

Richardson, Peter. *Herod King of the Jews and Friend of the Romans.* Minneapolis: Fortress, 1999. XXV + 360.

Roller, Duane W. *The Building Program of Herod the Great.* Berkeley: University of California Press, 1998. xvii + 352.

Sandmel, Samuel. *Herod: Profile of a Tyrant.* Philadelphia: Lippincott, 1967. 282 pp.

Stern, M. "The Reign of Herod and the Herodian Dynasty." *The Jewish People in the First Century.* Ed. S. Safrai and M. Stern. Philadelphia: Fortress, 1976. I, 216-307.

Westcott, Brooke Foss. "Herod." *Smith's Dictionary of the Bible.* Ed. H. B. Hackett. Grand Rapids: Baker; reprinted, 1971. II, 1048-1054.

5

JEWISH EXTRA— BIBLICAL LITERATURE

Alongside the canonical books of the Law, Prophets, and Writings, there was another body of literature referred to on occasion in the Old Testament. Included are such writings as the books of Jasher (Josh 10:13; 2 Sam 1:18), Nathan, Ahijah, and Iddo (2 Chron 9:29), Gad (1 Chron 29:29), Seraiah (2 Chron 12:15), Jehu (2 Chron 20:34), Isaiah's Acts of Uzziah (2 Chron 26:22), Jeremiah's Lamentation of Josiah (2 Chron 35:25), as well as many other of Solomon's psalms and proverbs (1 Kings 4:32), and several others (Num 21:14; 1 Sam 10:25; 1 Kings 11:41; 2 Chron 26:22). None of these writings were deemed necessary for inclusion into the Jewish canon--no doubt largely duplicating stories and events already portrayed in the canonical Scriptures.

However, *after* the completion of Malachi, the final book of the Old Testament, another quite secondary and confessedly *uninspired* group of books was written by Jewish writers. These books were composed largely between 180 B.C. and the time of Christ, some in Hebrew, and some in Greek. The two main bodies of this Jewish literature are the Apocrypha and the Pseudepigrapha, although additional writings have been discovered among the Dead Sea scrolls at Qumran.

I. THE APOCRYPHA

A. Why the Apocrypha Is Not Scripture

Even though the Roman Catholic Church voted to receive the fourteen books of the Apocrypha as genuinely inspired Scripture between 1542-60 at their Council of Trent, there are compelling reasons why the rest of the church did not. The Catholics wanted to find support for prayers for the dead, Jesuitical practices (the end justifies the means), the worship of angels, and other such patently false beliefs. They adopted these books during their Counter Reformation surge against Protestantism (Luther, Zwingli, Calvin, and the Anabaptists). To this day Catholic doctrine maintains and affirms an anathema (a curse that damns one to hell) on anyone who would deny that these books are inspired of God. Nevertheless, the rest of Christendom does not accept that proposition for the following reasons:

1. ***The Jews rejected the Apocrypha.*** Men like Ezra and those who followed him, even down to the Jewish discussions in Jamnia in A.D. 90, were in a far better position to judge the claims and worth of the Apocrypha than were the Jesuits coming out of the Dark Ages who were grasping for straws in a losing battle against Protestantism. Yet the Jews, then and today, do not recognize the Apocrypha as Scripture, but as mere *human* writings, set apart completely from the holy canon.

2. ***Christ and the Apostles never cited it.*** It is not an argument from silence but rather an

argument from extreme contrasts to note that Christ and the Apostles never cited from, nor alluded to any of the books of the Apocrypha. But the books of the canonical Old Testament were freely quoted and cited over and over again (Luke 24:27, 44).

3. *The Apocrypha is obviously not inspired.* There are numerous historical inaccuracies. For example, in Judith 1:5, 10 and 2:1, Nebuchadnezzar is called the King of the Assyrians, ruling in Ninevah! The death of Antiochus Epiphanes is given in two diverse ways in 2 Macc 1:15-17 and 9:5-29. One has him dying in the Temple (Jerusalem), while the other places his death in some far distant mountains in the east. In addition, false doctrines abound. Prayers, sacrifices, and offerings for the sins of the dead are taught (2 Macc 12:40-46). Contrast that with Heb 9:27 which teaches death followed by judgment. The pre-existence of the soul is found in Wisd Sol 8:19-20. Poor ethics abound as well--extolling lying, scheming, and murder, or any means that might justify the end (Jud 8-13).

4. *Their inspiration was denied.* Two well-known sources deny the inspiration of any books written during the time of the Apocrypha. (1) Josephus (*Against Apion* i.8) states that since the time of Artaxerxes the succession of the prophets ceased. There could be no Scripture without a true prophet. In addition, in the same passage, Josephus enumerates the canonical books, including only the thirty-nine found in our Old Testament today. (2) A second witness is 1 Macc 14:41. It records that the Jews "consented that he [Simon the brother of Judas Maccabeus] should be their prince, and high priest for ever, *till there should arise a faithful prophet*" (Emphasis

added). The obvious implication is that in 143 B.C. Israel had *no* faithful prophet. Hence, no genuine canonical Scripture could be written at that time.

B.   The Books of the Apocrypha

The fourteen books of the Apocrypha can be classified within four groups or headings. Only the briefest comments can accompany the mention of each book.

1.   *Additions to Canonical Books.* There are a number of additions to the canonical books such as: (1) Esth 10:4-16:34 consisting of extra prayers, legal proclamations, and embellished storytelling;   (2) Dan 3:24-90--the prayer of the three youths in the fire; Dan 13--Susanna; and Dan 14--Bel and the Dragon;   (3) parts of Ezra, Neh, and 2 Chron called 1 Esdras;   (4) the Prayer of Manasseh--15 verses in a group of odes following the Psalms which purports to be Manasseh's repentance (cf. 2 Chron 33:12-13).

2.   *Pseudepigraphical Writings.* Three books of the Apocrypha can be classed as pseudepigraphical writings. These are works that are falsely ascribed to someone else--in order to give them greater acceptance. These writings are: (1) Wisdom of Solomon--some 19 chapters of proverb-like material;   (2) Baruch--a 5 chapter work purported to be by the faithful scribe of Jeremiah;   (3) The Epistle of Jeremiah, 72 verses sometimes included as the sixth chapter of Baruch, is a letter as from Jeremiah to the captives in Babylon.

3.   *Legendary Stories.* Two books of the Apocrypha may be categorized as historical novels or legendary stories. These are: (1) Tobit, 14 chapters about a man's journey, marriage,

triumph over an evil demon, and recovery of money, and   (2) Judith, 16 chapters about a pretty and pious widow who cleverly chops off the head of the besieging general to save Jerusalem.

4. *Genuine and Authentic Treatises.* Several books of the Apocrypha are genuine authentic treatises--one being wisdom literature extolling right living according to the law and wisdom, and two others being treatises on the history of the Maccabean struggle. Ecclesiasticus, the wisdom literature, is unique in that the author's name is given--Jesus, son of Sirach, as well as hints as to the date, c. 180 B.C. Its 51 chapters also make it the longest book of the Apocrypha. 1 and 2 Maccabees, containing respectively 16 and 15 lengthy chapters, seem to recount the same history, but from a slightly differing viewpoint.

C. The Value of the Apocrypha

Altogether, the Apocrypha adds an additional one-seventh to the length of the Old Testament. The value of these books is chiefly that they provide insight into Jewish religious thinking and concerns--angels, demons, resurrection, the Law, moral living, God's help and intervention, and the value of prayer. A good history of the Maccabean period is afforded to posterity as well as glimpses into Jewish cultural and social development during the intertestamental period. Nevertheless, apart from their devotional value and interest appeal, they remain simply the works of men rather than the inspired Word of God.

II. THE PSEUDEPIGRAPHA

A. The Name and Value of the Pseudepigrapha

The Pseudepigrapha is a second group of Jewish intertestamental writings numbering about fifteen. As with the Apocrypha, these additional books help demonstrate the cultural, social, historical, and religious development of the Jews in the time just before the first coming of Christ. But, unlike the Apocrypha, the Pseudepigrapha is not considered to be Scripture by anyone--not even by the Catholic Church.

The title "Pseudepigrapha," (as in I.B.2 above), suggests that many of these writings were falsely ascribed to authors who did not actually produce them. The names of Isaiah, Enoch, Baruch, Ezra, Solomon, Moses, and even Adam and Eve are used in the various titles and in the literary structure of more than half of these books. This was meant to give the writings greater credibility and acceptance.

B. Classifications in the Pseudepigrapha

The books of the Pseudepigrapha are not easy to classify. As with the Apocrypha, some were originally composed in Hebrew or Aramaic, possibly in Palestine, while others perhaps came from Alexandria and were written in Greek. Scholars are still uncertain or divided about some. In addition, various *genres* or literary types are found, sometimes several different forms being exhibited within the same book. There is, however, a distinct emphasis on apocalypse--the concept of prophetic revelation often disclosed by means of visions. Perhaps most of the writings fall primarily into one of five categories, although some could doubtless fit into several groups.

1. ***Apocalypses.*** As just described, many of the writings contain some apocalyptic material, but several are *primarily* apocalypses, including (1) the Book of Enoch; (2) the Assumption of Moses; (3) the Apocalypse of Baruch; (4) the Ascension of Isaiah; and (5) IV Esdras. The Book of Enoch, for example, is set as the prophecy of Enoch about coming judgment and contains a large section about the Flood, a previous cataclysm. Also mentioned within its 108 chapters are fallen angels and giants--the latter of which were 3,000 cubits tall! That is a tall tale indeed. The Assumption of Moses has Moses tell Joshua the future of the Jews clear down to Herod's death!

2. ***Narratives and Legends.*** Some of the books are primarily set in narrative form mixed well with legend. Examples would be: (1) the Life of Adam and Eve and (2) Jubilees. Jubilees sets off earth's history in a series of Jubilees and recounts nearly the entire story of Genesis.

3. ***Testaments.*** There are a number of books set in the literary genre of a death-bed testament, that is, the final words uttered by one about to die. These are full of exhortation. They include: (1) The Testament of Adam (fragmentary); (2) The Testament of Abraham; (3) The Testament of Job; and (4) The Testament of the Twelve Patriarchs (the sons of Jacob). Some of these are lengthy, as Job's 51 chapters which are like a commentary on Job. But all are interesting and give rich and helpful insight into Jewish thinking.

Each of the twelve patriarchs, for example, looks back on some sin or vice in his own life and exhorts others to avoid it.

4. *Treatises.* Some of the books of the Pseudepigrapha are treatises on various subjects. (1) III Maccabees deals only with *conditions* similar to those of the Maccabees and hence gains its name. (2) IV Maccabees is a philosophical approach to the idea of reason. (3) The Sibylline Oracles, a group of 15 books, some Jewish (books 3-5), and some Christian, primarily treat the last days in oracular fashion. (4) The Letter of Aristeas concerns the origin of the Septuagint (LXX), the first Greek translation of the Hebrew Bible.

5. *Worship Hymns.* Two of the 150 Psalms are generally ascribed to Solomon--72 and 127. But the pseudepigraphous work, Psalms of Solomon, contains 18 more as from him. They are in many ways similar to the canonical psalms, but quite diverse as well. Nevertheless, they express the heart of a pious worshiper.

III. THE QUMRAN LITERATURE

A. The Qumran Community

In the centuries that preceded the coming of Christ an area near the Wadi Qumran at the northwest edge of the Dead Sea was used by Jewish religious groups. Known largely as the Essenes, these semi-monastic people copied not only the Scriptures, but also other, non-biblical works. Their community was later deserted, but many of their writings were sealed in jars and preserved in that dry climate in more than ten nearby caves. In 1947 a Bedouin shepherd came upon one of these caves, and suddenly the scrolls were discovered. More scrolls were found as archaeologists soon expanded the search over a larger area. Parts of every Old Testament book except Esther were found, copied with amazing accuracy. A brief listing of some of the main non-biblical works follows. Their importance, as with the Apocrypha and Pseudepigrapha, is that they disclose Jewish religious, cultural, and social development and give historical insights into the times.

B. The Qumran Writings

1. *The Manual of Discipline.* A document first called the Manual of Discipline was discovered in Cave 1, and later additional copies and fragments were found in Caves 3 and 4. The text concerns how the Qumran community was to live and order their existence with some apocalyptic glimpses into life in the future.

2. *The Damascus Document.* Originally discovered in Cairo in the late 1800's and named "Fragments of a Zadokite Work," the Damascus Document was found in multiple copies in Caves 4, 5, and 6 at Qumran. It deals with matters similar to those in the Manual of Discipline--rules and duties regarding their manner of life and religious practices, with a hint at an eschatological Messiah to come.

3. *The War Scroll.* Found in Cave 1, with fragments of four additional copies in Cave 4, this brief, 20 column writing depicts an eschatological war between the sons of Light and the sons of Darkness. It is, in fact, a detailed war manual and

presupposes a very activist climate among those
to be involved in the conflict.

4. ***Hymns and Prayers.*** A number of brief
works contain various hymns, prayers, and
psalms of thanksgiving. One short work is called
by the pseudepigraphous title of Psalms of
Joshua. They all similarly issue forth in praise to
God.

5. ***Commentaries.*** A number of Hebrew
commentaries, called *peshers*, have been
uncovered at Qumran. The most nicely written
one is a first century B.C. pesher on the Book of
Habakkuk, but others exist on the Psalms and
Isaiah as well as the minor prophets Hosea,
Micah, and Nahum. The comments often tell how
the verses apply to their daily life, or how they
were fulfilled in their recent Hasmonean history.

6. ***Apocalypses.*** Also found at Qumran are a
number of quite fragmentary works that are
apocalyptic in nature. One of these is a part of the
Book of Noah referred to in Jub 10:13 and 21:10.
Part of a Book of Secrets and several works related
to the Book of Enoch have also been discovered.

All of these non-biblical writings give us a
better idea of Jewish thought, hopes, and
expectations as the New Testament age was about
to dawn in Israel. Especially during the past forty
years since the discovery of the Dead Sea scrolls
(Qumran literature), more emphasis has rightly
been placed on these non-biblical sources as
important means for better understanding the
New Testament itself.

IV. FOR REVIEW AND DISCUSSION

1. What are the three main groups of extra-biblical Jewish literature written prior to the birth of Christ?

2. What types of literary forms or genre are to be found in the Apocrypha, Pseudepigrapha, and Qumran writings? Give examples of each category of writing.

3. Briefly describe to someone else the contents or "story" of some of these extra-biblical works.

4. Obtain a Catholic Bible or other copy of the Apocrypha and read several chapters of Tobit, Judith, 1 or 2 Macc, Bel and the Dragon, Susanna, or some other portion. After that first-hand experience how would you describe what you read? Was it interesting?

5. Why do we not accept the Apocrypha as inspired Scripture?

6. List the values that these extra-biblical sources possess. How can these works help one to better understand the New Testament?

V. FOR FURTHER READING AND RESEARCH

Bisell, Edwin Cone. *The Apocrypha of the Old Testament.* Ed. J. P. Lange. Trans. Philip Schaff. Vol. 15 of *Lange's Commentary on the Holy Scriptures.* New York: Scribner's, 1880. 680 pp.

Burrows, Millar. *The Dead Sea Scrolls.* New York: Viking, 1955. xxiv + 435.

Charles, Robert Henry. *The Apocrypha and Pseudepigrapha of the Old Testament in English.* Oxford: Clarendon Press; reprinted, 1963.

DeSilva, David Arthur. *Introducing the Apocrypha Message, Context, and Significance.* Grand Rapids, MI: Baker Academic, 2002. 428 pp.

Eissfeldt, Otto. *The Old Testament; An Introduction, Including the Apocrypha and Pseudepigrapha.* New York: Harper and Row, 1965. PP. 571-637.

Goodspeed, Edgar Johnson. *The Story of the Apocrypha.* Chicago, IL: The University of Chicago Press, 1939. ix + 150.

Harrison, R. K. *Introduction to the Old Testament.* Grand Rapids: Eerdmans, 1969. pp. 1175-1278.

Mansoor, Menahem. *The Dead Sea Scrolls.* Grand Rapids: Eerdmans, 1964. x + 210.

Metzger, Bruce Manning. *A Concordance to the Apocrypha/Deuterocanonical Books of the Revised Standard Version.* Grand Rapids: Eerdmans, 1983. 479 pp.

_____. *An Introduction to the Apocrypha.* New York: Oxford University Press, 1957. XII + 274.

Nickelsburg, George W. E. *Jewish Literature between the Bible and the Mishnah.* Philadelphia: Fortress Press, 1981. xx + 332.

Pfeiffer, Robert H. "The Literature and Religion of the Pseudepigrapha." *The Interpreter's Bible.* Ed. G. A. Buttrick. Nashville: Abingdon, 1952. pp. 421-436.

VanderKam, James C., and Peter W. Flint. *The Meaning of the Dead Sea Scrolls.* San Francisco: Harper-San Francisco, 2002. XII + 467.

6

CHRISTIAN APOCRYPHAL LITERATURE

I. INTRODUCTION

Luke begins his Gospel by saying that "many have taken in hand to set in order a narrative of those things which are most surely believed among us" (Luke 1:1). Apparently there were numerous feeble attempts by various writers to tell parts of the story about Jesus' life, ministry, death, and resurrection. However, only the four Gospels bear the marks of inspiration and are accepted as canonical. All other endeavors, however right their motives were, are uninspired, filled with errors, and laced through with imagination and fiction.

A. Definitions

The term *Christian apocryphal literature* means those writings of the Christian era that are clearly uninspired yet purport to give the life of Christ, the Apostles, or some epistles or apocalypses as by them. Hence, these writings are largely pseudepigraphical, that is, ascribed to someone who did not write them.

The word *apocryphal* connotes that which is false and spurious. The books to be considered below fall under their own weight of legend, congery, and uncurbed imagination. The Christian apocryphal literature is frequently not only spurious and absurd, but also heretical and impious.

B. Distinctions

There is a considerable body of literature written by known authors (in most cases) called the Church Fathers. They are sometimes divided into Apostolic Fathers (up to A.D. 100), Sub-Apostolic Fathers (A.D. 100-150), Apologists (A.D. 150-180), and so forth. All who wrote prior to the Council of Nicea in A.D. 325 are termed Ante-Nicene Fathers. Those living at the time of Nicea are called Nicene Fathers, and those after that time are the Post-Nicene Fathers. Men like Ignatius, Polycarp, Justin Martyr, Clement of Rome, Clement of Alexandria, Origen, Tertullian, Irenaeus and others were *legitimate writers* and their works are not to be confused with the *apocryphal* gospels, acts, epistles, and apocalypses mentioned in this chapter.

II. REASONS FOR APOCRYPHAL BOOKS

Man has an insatiable curiosity. Since each of the four canonical Gospels major on the public ministry, death, and resurrection of Christ, many wonder what His early life was like. Also, because the Acts of the Apostles concludes with Paul in prison in Rome, we want to know what happened after that. Likewise, since only Matthew and John (as Apostles) wrote Gospels, what did the others have to say? What about Andrew, Bartholomew, Philip, Simon, James, and a few other famous names like Nicodemus and Joseph of Arimathea? We wonder what Pilate would have to say. Could not the gaps be filled in somewhat? The result is what we possess today known as Christian apocryphal literature. Much of it was circulating in the 2nd and 3rd centuries, although even more was composed much later on in a type of parasitic plagiarism. Some of these books are mentioned in the next section.

III. TYPES OF CHRISTIAN APOCRYPHAL BOOKS

As with the New Testament, the apocryphal literature groups itself easily under four headings. Gospels tell about some aspects of Christ's life. Acts usually deal with the lives of the Apostles, and Epistles pretend to be letters--usually by an Apostle or someone else close to Christ. Lastly, there are, just as in Jewish literature, apocalypses.

A. Gospels

There are about fifty apocryphal gospels of various types. Their purposes are generally either (1) to forward some heresy; or (2) to supplement the life of Christ. Under the first category would be a number of Ebionite or Jewish-type gospels, plus some obviously Gnostic gospels. The Ebionite gospels had names including the word Hebrews or Nazarenes in their titles, and are known only from occasional quotes and obscure references in the Church Fathers. Another early fragmentary work is the Gospel of the Egyptians of which only three verses remain.

Some of these apocryphal gospels (1) treat the *nativity*, as do the Protevangelium of James (25 chapters), Pseudo-Matthew, the Nativity of Mary, and the Passing of Mary. (2) Others deal with the *childhood* of Jesus as do the Gospel of Thomas and an Arabic Gospel of the childhood. (3) A third class covers the *passion and resurrection* of the Lord as, for example, the Gospel of Nicodemus.

There are gospels attributed to each of the following persons: Nazarenes, Ebionites, Hebrews, Egyptians, Peter, Philip, Thomas, Matthias, Judas, James, Bartholomew, the Twelve, the Seventy, Nicodemus, and even Gamaliel. Gnostic gospels were written by Cerinthus, Basilides, Marcion, Apelles, Bardesanes, and Mani. Others are purported to be dialogues with Jesus or with Mary.

The infancy Gospel of Thomas tells of certain boyhood miracles Jesus performed. These include killing several other boys who exasperated Jesus, raising the dead, causing clay pigeons to become alive and fly away, lengthening a board that Joseph had cut off too short, and so forth. But John 2:11 reports that the miracle at Cana (water to wine) was the "beginning of signs" that Jesus performed. If that be the case, then all previous signs are completely ficticious.

B. Acts

The acts of various Apostles form a second group of the Christian apocryphal literature. The primary books are those about John, Paul, Peter, Andrew, and Thomas, although there is one titled Later Acts of Other Apostles which includes Philip, Matthew, Bartholomew, Simon and Judas, Thaddaeus, and Barnabas. They partake of a certain amount of romance rather than history, and often reflect later ascetic ideals. There is usually a journey involved and certain exciting encounters, such as talking animals, cannibals, sorcerers, kings, beautiful women and so forth. There is also an interest in legend and a delight in the miraculous.

C. Epistles

The apocryphal epistles are fewer in number than either the gospels or the acts. They follow a similar format to the New Testament epistles and sometimes have an apologetic purpose as with the Epistles of Paul and Seneca (the Roman philosopher). The Gospel to the Laodiceans was no doubt suggested by the reference to "the epistle from Laodicea" (Col 4:16). Perhaps because Clement of Rome, an early church father, penned a real Epistle to the Corinthians (A.D. 96), someone else got the idea too and wrote the Third Epistle to the Corinthians. Other titles are The Epistles of Christ and Abgarus, The Epistles of the Apostles, and The Apocryphal Epistle of Titus.

D. Apocalypses

A fourth category of apocryphal Christian work takes the apocalypse genre. This vision-type literature is attributed to James, Paul, Peter, Stephen, Thomas, and even the Virgin (Mary). They frequently discuss heaven, hell, judgment, and the end of the world. Peter, for example, gives a personal tour of the torments of hell, and Paul tells what was revealed to him when he was "caught up to the third heaven . . . caught up into Paradise" (2 Cor 12:2-4).

IV.   THE NAG HAMMADI LITERATURE

In 1946, an ancient library was discovered about forty miles northwest of Luxor in Upper Egypt (up the Nile means going south). There were 13 codices (a codex is a book-form manuscript), containing 45 different treatises on 794 pages--all in the Coptic language (very similar to Greek). Originating from the 3rd and 4th centuries A.D., these Gnostic Christian writings contained explanations of the beginnings of the world (cosmogonies), gospels, epistles, apocalypses, and prayers.

The immense discovery bolstered earlier finds farther north at Oxyrhynchus (120 miles south of Cairo) by Grenfell and Hunt from 1896 to 1906. In both cases the writings were on papyrus. Interestingly enough, the most fruitful discoveries are often made in trash heaps where these types of materials have been discarded!

V.   THE VALUE OF CHRISTIAN APOCRYPHAL LITERATURE

One of the values of any literature is that it reveals the hopes, imaginations, and likes and dislikes of its author. These works are no exception to that rule--especially in the area of imagination. Very little, if any, historical facts are contained in these works, but they do show the theology of the Gnostics first hand in the Nag Hammadi library. The growing veneration of Mary, Joseph, and some of the Apostles is also demonstrated.

But the greatest value these works possess is probably seen by comparing them with the actual New Testament itself. By comparison, the apocryphal books fade away. Their fiction is plainly seen in contrast with the level historical accounts found in the Gospels.

They speak a word about canonicity too. The apocryphal writings circulated among Christians and were read and evaluated. Not one was ever considered canonical or inspired. Those who knew and judged the evidence first hand found those apocryphal sources wanting. Nevertheless, they are interesting fiction to say the least.

VI.   FOR REVIEW AND DISCUSSION

1. Distinguish between Apocrypha and apocryphal.
2. Describe the characteristics of apocryphal Christian literature.
3. Make a distinction between the Church Fathers and the apocryphal writings of the same period.
4. Why were apocryphal works written?
5. List and describe four primary types of Christian apocryphal literature. Can you name a few books from each category?
6. Where have many of the discoveries of the texts in question been made? Does the dry climate of that region of the world have anything to do with preservation?
7. What values do these false books possess?

VII.   FOR FURTHER READING AND RESEARCH

Bock, Darrell L. *Breaking the Da Vinci Code: Answers to the Questions Everyone's Asking.* Waterville, ME: Thorndike Press, 2004. 239 pp.

_____. *Jesus According to Scripture: Restoring the Portrait from the Gospels*. Grand Rapids: Baker, 2002. 704 pp.

Davies, T. W. "Apocrypha." *The International Standard Bible Encyclopedia*. Ed. G. W. Bromiley. Grand Rapids: Eerdmans, 1979. I, 161-165.

Ehrman, Bart D. *Lost Christianities: The Battle for Scripture and the Faiths We Never Knew*. New York: Oxford University Press, 2003. xv + 294.

Enslin, Morton Scott. "NT Apocrypha." *The Interpreter's Dictionary of the Bible*. Ed. G. A. Buttrick. Nashville: Abingdon, 1962. I, 166-169.

Findlay, Adam Fyfe and Andrew F. Walls. "Apocryphal Acts." *The International Standard Bible Encyclopaedia*. Ed. G. W. Bromiley. Grand Rapids: Eerdmans, 1979. I, 165-173.

Helmbold, Andrew K. *The Nag Hammadi Gnostic Texts and the Bible*. Grand Rapids: Baker, 1967.

James, Montague Rhodes. *The Apocryphal New Testament*. Oxford: Clarendon, 1955.

Pagels, Elaine H. *Beyond Belief: The Secret Gospel of Thomas*. New York: Random House, 2003. 241 pp.

Robinson, James McConkey. Ed. *The Nag Hammadi Library in English*. 4th rev. ed. Leiden: Brill, 1996.

Schneemelcher, Wilhelm, and R. McL.Wilson. *New Testament Apocrypha*. Cambridge [England]: J. Clarke & Co, 1991.

Trebilco, Paul R. *The Early Christians in Ephesus from Paul to Ignatius*. Tübingen: Mohr Siebeck, 2004.

Walls, Andrew F. "Apocryphal Apocalypses." *The International Standard Bible Encyclopedia*. Ed. G. W. Bromiley. Grand Rapids: Eerdmans, 1979. I, 173-181.

Yamauchi, Edwin M. "Apocryphal Gospels." *The International Standard Bible Encyclopedia*. Ed. G. W. Bromiley. Grand Rapids: Eerdmans, 1979. I, 181-188.

7

JEWISH SECTS AND GROUPS

One does not read far into the New Testament before he comes upon groups and institutions known as Pharisees, Sadducees, Herodians, Elders, Sanhedrin, and synagogue. But in addition to these are the Essenes, Zealots, Sicarii, lawyers, scribes, publicans--terms with which the average reader may not be familiar. What were the primary beliefs, practices, and functions of these groups? How do they fit into the overall New Testament picture?

I. RELIGIOUS SECTS

For some time before, during, and after the birth and ministry of Jesus Christ there were three primary religious sects in Palestinian Judaism. Although none of the three groups were large in numbers, they each made lasting impressions on their immediate generations. The largest of the three major religious parties was the Pharisees.

A. The Pharisees

The Pharisees are first mentioned as a religious party during the reign of John Hyrcanus

(135-105 B.C.). Their spiritual predecessors, the Hasidim, supported the Maccabean efforts to oppose Hellenization in Israel. Their name signifies being separated. Their primary emphasis was a strict adherence to legalistic tradition. Apparently, this led some Pharisees to place outward conformity to the Law above inward matters of the heart, a tendency that both Isaiah and Jesus decried (Isa 58:1-9; Matt 15:1-20). Although the Pharisees may have numbered less than 5,000, they used the synagogue to teach the people their strict legalism. They are to be admired for holding strong religious convictions even when such was not always popular.

Doctrinally, several beliefs distinguished the Pharisees from their counterpart, the Sadducees. The Pharisees believed (1) in foreordination, that God divinely controlled history, but that man's free will was not impaired; (2) in the immortality of the soul, future rewards and punishments, and the resurrection of the body for life on earth with the Messiah; (3) in personal angels and demons; (4) in both the written law and in the oral tradition surrounding it--both as *equally* authoritative and binding; and (5) in a Messiah who would overthrow the Gentiles and drive them out (Josephus, *Antiq.* xviii.1.3; Acts 23:8).

John the Baptist had termed both the Pharisees and Sadducees a "brood of vipers" (Luke 3:7), and Jesus warned his disciples of their "leaven" or teaching (Matt 16:6; 11-12). To gain entrance into heaven, Jesus said, one's righteousness would need to *exceed* that of the Pharisees (Matt 5:20). Jesus severely denounced the Pharisees in Matt 23:1-39 during crucifixion week. However, they had plotted His death for years (Mark 3:6; John 11:47-57). Jesus did not fit their expectations of a Messiah, and they rejected His claims of deity (Luke 5:21).

B. The Sadducees

Whereas the Pharisees came primarily from the middle class, the Sadducees were the aristocracy of their day. The priesthood was frequently occupied by a Sadducee (Acts 5:17), relating back to their claimed connection with Zadok, the priest in David's reign whose descendants continued in the office until Maccabean times. The Sadducees were an exclusive group--usually sophistocated, wealthy landowners--centered around Jerusalem. They were rigidly conservative in wanting to preserve what they had. Their political power increased during the Seleucid days as they maneuvered for power opposite their Pharisee rivals.

Theologically, they differed with the Pharisees on several key issues. Primarily, they accepted only the Scriptures without giving weight to any so-called traditions that orally accompanied the Law. In addition, they denied the soul's immortality and the resurrection of the body (Matt 22:23-33), believing instead that Sheol was simply the grave. Since resurrection is taught in the Old Testament (Job 19:26; Ps 16:10; Dan 12:2), it is thought that the Sadducees must have subordinated all other Old Testament writings to those of Moses.

The Sadducees opposed the Pharisees, but were united with them against Jesus (Matt 16:1-12), and against the Apostles, chiefly because the Sadducees disagreed with the teaching about resurrection (Matt 22:23-33; Acts 4:1-3; 5:17-18).

C. The Essenes

The Essenes, although not mentioned in the New Testament, are referred to by Philo, Pliny, and Josephus (*Antiq.* xviii.1.5). They numbered perhaps less than 5,000 and lived primarily in communal arrangements in Judea and in the Qumran area. They were quite scrupulous and pious in their religion, attending to washings, baptisms, prayer, reading and copying the Scriptures, swearing to keep the Sabbath and the Law till death. In fact, their name means pious or holy. A two to three year probation was required before one could join, and then all property was given over to the group. Meals were taken in common, and no presents could be received from outsiders. All worship was confined to their community setting, since the Essenes felt the Temple was polluted. The Essenes were the producers of the Dead Sea scrolls--including the Manual of Discipline and the War Scroll which reveal much about their conduct and worship.

II. RELIGIOUS AND POLITICAL INSTITUTIONS

A. The Synagogue

The synagogue was a Jewish place for worship. It is believed that the practice began during the Babylonian Captivity (605-538 B.C.) when the Temple was destroyed and the people were removed from the land. In Christ's day it also served as the local law court and the school where boys learned to read the Torah. The synagogue was governed by a group of elders with special officers appointed--such as a ruler who presided and appointed others to read the Scriptures and speak (Mark 5:35-38; Luke 8:41, 49; 13:14; Acts 18:8, 17).

Jesus frequently preached in the synagogues (Matt 4:23; Luke 4:16), as did Paul and Barnabas on their missionary journeys (Acts 13:14-16, 44; 14:1; 17:1-2, 10; 18:4). The Apostles *reached* the Jews in the synagogue on the sabbath, but when Christian congregations were established, worship was on Sunday, the *first* day of the week (Acts 20:7; 1 Cor 16:1-2).

B. The Sanhedrin

The highest Jewish governmental body in the time of Christ and the Apostles was the Sanhedrin. The term used in most English versions is *the Council* (Matt 26:59; Acts 4:5-6, 15; 5:21, 27; 6:12; 22:30). It was composed of seventy members to correspond with the seventy elders Moses appointed (Num 11:16, 24). The high priest acted as its president and was the seventy-first member.

When Herod seized control of Israel by 37 B.C., he killed forty-five members of the Sanhedrin and appointed men he could control (*Antiq.* xiv.9.4; xv.1.2). In Christ's time the Sanhedrin had the power over life and death but had to submit such decisions to Roman authority (John 18:31; 19:6-11). Jesus was, of course, tried by the Sanhedrin (Mark 14:55), as were Peter and John and the other Apostles (Acts 4:5-6, 15; 5:21, 27), Stephen (Acts 6:12) and Paul (Acts 22:30; 23:1-10). It seems that Nicodemus and Joseph of Arimathea were both members of the Council (Luke 23:50; John 3:1). With the destruction of Jerusalem by the Romans in A.D. 70, the activity of the Sanhedrin ceased.

III. SMALLER GROUPS

A number of other smaller, yet influential groups are mentioned in the New Testament. A brief knowledge of each group will aid in one's understanding of the New Testament.

A. Zealots

The Zealots were a small group that maintained the spiritual heritage of the Maccabees. They opposed giving tribute to Caesar and refused to pay taxes. Starting with the rebellion of Judas the Galilean in A.D. 6 (Acts 5:37; *Antiq.* xx.5.2; *Wars* ii.8.1), they pledged unconditional obedience to God and undying opposition to Rome. They were active in the war of rebellion in A.D. 66-70 and fled to Masada after Jerusalem's fall. Their suicide pact is recorded by Josephus (*Wars* vii.9). Another branch of the Zealots was called the *sicarii*, or assassins, who caused great trouble for Rome (*Wars* vii.10.1). Jesus apparently chose a Zealot (Simon) for one of His disciples (Luke 6:15; Acts 1:13).

B. Herodians

The Herodians were a Jewish group who supported the family rule of the Herods in Israel. Their policy was to please Rome as well. They combined with the Pharisees in Galilee to plot Jesus' death (Mark 3:6), and in Jerusalem they sought by trickery to make Jesus appear to be either a traitor to Israel or to Rome (Matt 22:16; Mark 12:13). In the New Testament they are mentioned in only the three references cited above.

C. Chief Priests, Elders, and Rulers

More than sixty times in the Gospels and Acts one reads of the chief priests, usually in conjunction with the scribes, elders, and on occasion the Pharisees. Chief priests probably denotes the high priest, ex-high priests, and other Temple rulers and those set over the treasury of the Temple. They were important individuals who sat on the Sanhedrin. Their opposition to Jesus was great, and they devised the scheme with Judas Iscariot that led to Jesus' betrayal and arrest (Matt 26:3-4, 14-16, 47, 57).

The priesthood, after the Hasmonean age, was neither hereditary nor for life-long tenure. It became a political office with Herod and the Romans, and this is amply reflected in the events of the Gospels and Acts. The terms elders and rulers typically refer to other senior members of society who often sat on the Jewish Council (Sanhedrin).

D. Scribes and Lawyers

Lawyers, mentioned seven times in the Gospels (six in Luke, and once in Matt), were professional interpreters of the Law of Moses. Scribes, found sixty-one times in the Gospels and three times in Acts, copied the Law of Moses, but are identical with those termed lawyers (cf. Matt 22:35 and Mark 12:28). They dealt with Moses' Law, but in such a way as to pervert its true meaning at times. They came under severe criticism from Christ especially in Luke 11:44-52 where Jesus denounced the lawyers, and in Matt 23:2, 13-15, 23, 25, 27, and 29 where those termed scribes are castigated. They regularly plotted against Jesus together with the chief priests, elders, rulers, and the entire Sanhedrin (Matt 23:3).

E. Publicans

Just as scribes and lawyers are names of occupations, so is that of publican. Publicans were tax collectors--for Rome--and hence despised by many Jews. They were classified with harlots (Luke 18:11), sinners (Mark 2:16), and others of low esteem. Jesus was accused of eating with them and of being their friend (Mark 2:16; Luke 7:34), definitely a calculated slur. Yet Jesus chose Levi or "Matthew the tax collector" (Matt 10:3) to be one of the Apostles, and He took special interest in the salvation of Zacchaeus who was "a chief tax collector" (Luke 19:2, 9-10). The publicans thronged to hear John the Baptist and Jesus (Luke 3:12; 5:29; 15:1), and no doubt many were saved as was the publican in Jesus' parable (Luke 18:9-14).

IV.   FOR REVIEW AND DISCUSSION

1.   What are the chief characteristics and/or contributions of the three primary religious sects of the Jews during Christ's day?
2.   Discuss with someone else Jesus' attitude and relationship to these three groups.
3.   What was the composition and function of the synagogue and the Sanhedrin in first century Jewish society? What contact did Christ and the early Apostles have with these two institutions?
4.   Be able to list, define, and discuss the nature of the other smaller groups in Jewish society covered in section III above. How important was each group and how did they each relate to Jesus?

V. FOR FURTHER READING AND RESEARCH

Abrahams, Israel. *Studies in Pharisaism and the Gospels.* New York: Ktav, 1967.

Brandon, S. G. F. *Jesus and the Zealots.* Manchester: University of Manchester Press, 1967. xvi + 413.

Evans, Craig A. and Stanley E. Porter, Eds. *Dictionary of New Testament Background.* Downers Grove, IL: InterVarsity, 2000. xxxiv + 1328.

Green, Joel B. and Scot McKnight. *Dictionary of Jesus and the Gospels.* Downers Grove, IL: InterVarsity, 1992. xxvi + 933.

Hagner, Donald A. "Pharisees." *The Zondervan Pictorial Encyclopedia of the Bible.* Ed. M. C. Tenney. Grand Rapids: Zondervan, 1975. IV, 745-752.

_____. "Sadducees." *The Zondervan Pictorial Encyclopedia of the Bible.* Ed. M. C. Tenney. Grand Rapids: Zondervan, 1975. V, 211-216.

Jeremias, Joachim. *Jerusalem in the Time of Jesus.* Trans. F. H. and C. H. Cave. Philadelphia: Fortress, 1975. xvi + 405.

Josephus. *Antiquities.* xiii.5.9; xiii.10.6; xviii.5.3-6. *Wars.* i.5.2; ii.8.2, 14; iv.3-11.

Martin, Ralph P. and Peter H. Davids. *Dictionary of the Later New Testament & Its Developments.* Downers Grove, IL: InterVarsity, 1997. xxx + 1289.

Metzger, Bruce Manning. *The New Testament Its Background, Growth, and Content.* 3rd Rev. Ed. Nashville: Abingdon, 2003. 370 pp.

Moore, George Foot. *Judaism in the First Centuries of the Christian Era.* Cambridge: Harvard University Press, 1962. 3 vols.

Robertson, A. T. *The Pharisees and Jesus: The Stone Lectures for 1915-16, Delivered at the Princeton Theological Seminary.* Eugene, OR: Wipf and Stock, 1999. xii + 189.

8

KEYS TO
NEW TESTAMENT
CHRONOLOGY

The purpose of this chapter is not to solve all of the problems of New Testament chronology, but to raise the pertinent questions and to supply some facts and Scriptures that may suggest a framework for possible answers. The two areas covered are   (1) the dates connected with the life of Christ; and   (2) the chronology of the Book of Acts.

I. DATING THE LIFE OF CHRIST

Five events or periods in the life of Christ provide a fertile area for chronological research and speculation. They are   (1) the date of Christ's birth;   (2) the year Jesus' ministry began;   (3) the length of Christ's ministry;   (4) the day of the crucifixion; and   (5) the year of the crucifixion.

A. The Date of Christ's Birth

Several factors are involved in determining the date of Christ's birth (meaning which *year*. The *day* of the year, traditionally December 25, may or may not be exact). (1) Jesus obviously was born while Herod the Great was still alive (Matt 2:1-16) and was probably some months old before the wise men arrived from the east. Mary and Joseph were then living in a house, not a manger (Matt 2:11). Josephus tells us that Herod died in the 37th year of his reign (*Antiq.* xvii.7.1; *Wars* i.23.8), and that there was a lunar eclipse in Palestine shortly before his death which immediately preceded the Passover. The eclipse probably occurred on March 12 or 13 of 4 B.C. Jesus, therefore, could have been born in 4 or 5 B.C., or perhaps earlier since Herod sought to kill all infants two and under (Matt 2:16). (2) Another factor, no doubt less precise, is the indication that an initial census or registration was taking place at the time while Quirinius was governing Syria. He was a military governor of Syria beginning about 8 or 7 B.C., so Christ's birth could not have been before that.

Questions often arise about how Christ could be born in 4 B.C. (*before* Christ). In about A.D. 525, Dionysius Exiguus, a Roman abbot, devised the system of centering the world's history around Christ. Later, however, it was discovered that Dionysius had omitted four years of history which then had to be reinserted, thus pushing Christ's birth back as well.

B. The Beginning of Christ's Ministry

The considerations bearing on the time when Christ began His public ministry are several. (1) Luke 3:23 says that Jesus "began His ministry at about thirty years of age." If He was born in 4 or 5 B.C., that would make it A.D. 25 or 26. But the flexibility of the Greek word *hosi* (about), is debated. Some feel there may be a two to three year latitude, while others do not.   (2) Luke 3:1 places the beginning of Jesus' public ministry in the 15th year of the reign of Tiberius Caesar. Since his rule commenced in about A.D. 14, a date of A.D. 29 might fit.   (3) When Jesus cleansed the Temple during the first Passover of His ministry, the Jews remarked that "It has taken forty-six years to build this Temple" (John 2:20). The Temple was begun by Herod in 19 or 20 B.C. which would date Christ's initial ministry at about A.D. 26.

C.   The Length of Christ's Ministry

The length of Christ's ministry can only be determined from John's Gospel where three Passovers are specifically mentioned (2:13; 6:4; and 11:55). It is felt that an additional fourth Passover might be found in John 5:1 "a feast of the Jews," or else in 4:35 which says that harvest time was only four months away, meaning that another Passover was almost upon them. Four Passovers would yield a three year plus ministry. The three synoptic Gospels, Matt, Mark, and Luke, mention only Christ's *final* Passover when He was crucified in Jerusalem.

D.   The Day of the Crucifixion

Most Christians celebrate Christ's crucifixion on a Friday, although a few believe it occurred on a Wednesday, and some that it happened on a Thursday.

(1) The *Wednesday view* is based almost entirely on a forced literal application of Matt 12:40 which says that "the Son of Man will be three days and three nights in the heart of the earth." This view requires burial at precisely sundown on Wednesday, and the resurrection at

precisely sundown on Saturday to insure three exact days and three exact nights in the tomb--no more, and no less. Such a view seems extreme, quite unconventional, and ignores other clear texts--such as Matt 16:21, 17:23, and 20:19 where Jesus said He would rise again "the third day," not *after* three complete days and three complete nights.

(2) The *Thursday view* cites John 19:31 in an attempt to prove that Friday and Saturday were *both* sabbaths during that holy week. Lev 16:29, 31 do declare that particular feast days could be sabbaths in addition to the usual Saturday sabbath, but that does not establish this view.

(3) The traditional *Friday view* seems to fit the evidence best. First, Luke 23:56 says that the women saw Jesus buried, then went home to prepare spices and "they rested on the Sabbath according to the commandment." *The commandment* is a clear reference to the *fourth* commandment (Exod 20:9-11) which can only refer to Saturday as the day after the crucifixion. The very next verse in Luke (24:1) says "Now on the first day of the week." They rested Saturday and came back early Sunday morning. A Wednesday crucifixion, for example, must maintain that the women rested Thursday, *and* Friday, *and* Saturday (*three* full days of rest) before their return to the tomb on Sunday. Secondly, notice that the two on the road to Emmaus plainly stated that Sunday was "the third day since these things happened" (Luke 24:21). The Jews always included the day something happened as the first day in reckoning time from that event. Thus, a week after the crucifixion was referred to as "after eight days" (John 20:26). If Sunday was the third day, then the event must have occurred on Friday. If the

crucifixion had been on Wednesday, they would have said it was the fifth day since it had happened.

E. The Year of the Crucifixion

The year of Christ's crucifixion is primarily reckoned by adding the length of His ministry to the time when it began. The views range in extremes from A.D. 21 to 36, but it seems best to see a date between A.D. 29 and 33. The date of the crucifixion must also fit in chronologically with the key points in the history outlined in the Book of Acts.

II. THE CHRONOLOGY OF ACTS

There are several rather fixed points where the chronology of the Book of Acts intersects with the history of the Roman world. It is from these dates that the rest of New Testament chronology is constructed.

A. The Death of Herod Agrippa I

Acts 12:3, 19 and 23 place the death of Herod Agrippa I in the spring of the year, just after the Passover. The Jewish historian, Josephus, says that he died during his *seventh year* of rule which would have been A.D. 44 (*Antiq.* xviii.7.1; xix.8.2; *Wars* ii.9.6; ii.11.6). The death of James, the brother of John, also coincided with that of Herod Agrippa I (Acts 12:2-3).

B. The Famine Under Claudius

In Antioch, a Christian prophet named Agabus predicted a famine would occur during the reign of Claudius (Acts 11:28). The approach of that famine is tied to the death of Herod Agrippa I in A.D. 44 by Acts 11:30 and 12:25. Josephus mentions a famine in Palestine during the rule of the procurators Fadus and Alexander who were in office from A.D. 44-48 (*Antiq.* xx.2.5). As a result, Paul's famine visit is usually placed around A.D. 46.

C. Gallio's Proconsulship in Corinth

Gallio, the brother of Seneca, spent one year in Corinth as the proconsul of Achaia (Acts 18:12-16). An inscription from Delphi during the reign of Claudius mentions Gallio with the number 26 for its date. Beginning in August of A.D. 52, the number 27 was used on Claudius' inscriptions. The term of a proconsul was for one year, and Gallio only served one time. Since Paul was brought before Gallio by the Jews in a complaint, Paul's 18 month stay in Corinth on the second missionary journey can be dated between about A.D. 50-53.

D. Festus as Procurator of Judea

Acts 24:27 records that Festus became procurator of Judea after Paul had been imprisoned in Caesarea under Felix for two years. Festus replaced Felix, who had been appointed by Claudius in A.D. 52. When Paul was first imprisoned he spoke of Felix as having been "for many years a judge of this nation" (Acts 24:10). If Felix was replaced two years later in A.D. 60, then the "many years" Paul alluded to would have been the six years from A.D. 52-58. Festus' rule was shorter than that of Felix, because his successor Albinus was in place in A.D. 62. If Paul's

Caesarean imprisonment was from A.D. 58-60, then his first Roman imprisonment must have been between A.D. 60-62 (Acts 28:30).

E.   The Conversion and Life of Paul

The Book of Acts and Paul's thirteen recognized epistles give clues as to the chronology of the life of that great Apostle. The dating of most of Paul's epistles hinges on these chronological keys as well.

1. *Paul's Conversion.* The story of Paul's conversion is recounted in Acts 9, 22, and 26, and more light is thrown on the chronology surrounding that event in Gal 1:17-2:20, Acts 11:27-30, and in Acts 15:1-35. Saved just outside Damascus, Paul remained in that city and in the nearby Arabian desert for the next three years (Acts 9:20-22; Gal 1:17), after which time he left Damascus and visited Jerusalem for the first time since his conversion (Acts 9:23-28; Gal 1:18-19). Then, after 14 years (presumably 14 years after his conversion), he revisited Jerusalem again as explained in Gal 2:1-10.

2. *Famine Visit or Jerusalem Council?* The material related about the Gal 2 visit to Jerusalem might fit either of two different trips--that of a famine visit (Acts 11:27-30), or that of the Jerusalem Council (Acts 15:1-35). I feel that Gal 2 corresponds with the famine visit for the following reasons: (1) the famine visit would have been Paul's *second* visit to Jerusalem and Gal 2:1 indicates it was his second trip there.   (2) Acts 11 and Gal 2 speak of *private* discussions not general church meetings with the elders and other members present (cf. Gal 2:2; Acts 15:6, 22).   (3) Paul said he went up to Jerusalem "by revelation"

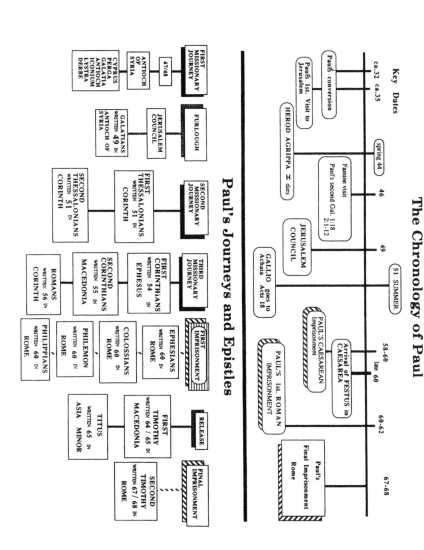

The Chronology of Paul

Key Dates

ca.32 ca.35	Paul's conversion
	Paul's 1st Visit to Jerusalem
	HEROD AGRIPPA II dies
spring 44	
46	Famine visit — Paul's second Gal. 1:18 2:1-12
49	JERUSALEM COUNCIL
51 SUMMER	GALLIO goes to Achaia Acts 18
58-60	PAUL'S CAESAREAN Imprisonment
late 60	Arrival of FESTUS in CAESAREA
	PAUL'S 1st ROMAN IMPRISONMENT
60-62	
67-68	Paul's Final Imprisonment Rome

Paul's Journeys and Epistles

FIRST MISSIONARY JOURNEY

ANTIOCH OF SYRIA → CYPRUS PERGA GALATIA ANTIOCH ICONIUM LYSTRA DERBE

47/48

FURLOUGH

JERUSALEM COUNCIL → ANTIOCH OF SYRIA

GALATIANS WRITTEN 49 IN

SECOND MISSIONARY JOURNEY

FIRST THESSALONIANS WRITTEN 51 IN CORINTH

SECOND THESSALONIANS WRITTEN 51 IN CORINTH

THIRD MISSIONARY JOURNEY

FIRST CORINTHIANS WRITTEN 54 IN EPHESUS

SECOND CORINTHIANS WRITTEN 55 IN MACEDONIA

ROMANS WRITTEN 56 IN CORINTH

FIRST IMPRISONMENT

EPHESIANS WRITTEN 60 IN ROME

COLOSSIANS WRITTEN 60 IN ROME

PHILEMON WRITTEN 60 IN ROME

PHILIPPIANS WRITTEN 60 IN ROME

RELEASE

FIRST TIMOTHY WRITTEN 64 / 65 IN MACEDONIA

TITUS WRITTEN 65 IN ASIA MINOR

FINAL IMPRISONMENT

SECOND TIMOTHY WRITTEN 67 / 68 IN ROME

(Gal 2:2), which conforms to the revelation given by Agabus in Acts 11:27-30.   (4) In both Acts 11:30 and in Gal 2:1 only two messengers were sent from Antioch to Jerusalem--Paul and Barnabas. Titus was only subordinate in Gal 2, but by contrast Acts 15 suggests that a number of other messengers were deputized along with Paul and Barnabas.   (5) In Gal 2 no question was posed to the church and no official answer was given. This fits better with the Acts 11 famine visit than the Acts 15 Jerusalem Council which drafted an official statement on their decision (Acts 15:22-29).

What bearing does the above discussion have on the chronology of the New Testament? Simply this. If Gal 2 and Acts 11 are to be equated, then Paul was saved 14 years before A.D. 46--meaning A.D. 32. If, as some maintain, Gal 2 and Acts 15 correspond, then Paul was saved in A.D. 35.

3. *Paul's Journeys and Epistles.* In either case, Paul's *first* missionary journey to Galatia (with Barnabas, Acts 13-14) must have taken place after the famine visit of A.D. 46 (Acts 11:30; 12:25), and prior to the Jerusalem Council of A.D. 49. Shortly after that journey and before the Council of A.D. 49, Paul may have written Galatians as his first epistle.

Paul's *second* journey took him through Galatia again and on to Europe--Philippi, Thessalonica, Berea, Athens, and Corinth (Acts 15:40-16:22). Since he spent 18 months in Corinth itself (Acts 18:11), the entire trip probably covered A.D. 50-53. Only two letters, 1 and 2 Thess, dated A.D. 51-52, were written on that trip.

Paul's *third* journey went through Galatia and on to Ephesus where he spent three years (Acts 18:23-21:8; cf. 20:31). This trip must have consumed most of A.D. 53-57. From Ephesus, Paul wrote 1 and 2 Cor (A.D. 54-55), and then from

Corinth or nearby Cenchrea, Paul wrote to the Roman believers in A.D. 57 (Rom 16:1; cf. Acts 20:1-3).

Paul spent A.D. 58-60 imprisoned in Caesarea until he appealed his case to Caesar (Acts 25:11-12). After his shipwreck and trip to Rome, Paul waited two years in Rome for his case to be heard by Nero (A.D. 60-62). During that time Paul penned four "prison" epistles--Col, Philem, Eph, and Phil. But it is important to remember that Paul was guarded during those two years "in his owned rented house," not in some dungeon (Acts 28:30).

After his release, Paul may have gone to Colossae (Philem 22), and then off to Spain (Rom 15:28). Eventually, he evangelized Crete (Titus 1:5), wintered at Nicopolis in Greece (Titus 3:12), passed through Miletus (2 Tim 4:20), and was later captured and taken to Rome for his execution. Before his final arrest, he wrote 1 Tim and Titus (A.D. 64-65). During his final imprisonment (in the Mamertine Prison) in Rome, Paul sent Timothy his final letter (2 Tim, A.D. 65-66). If Paul wrote the Book of Heb, it must have been before his final imprisonment when he was still free to travel (Heb 13:23).

III. FOR REVIEW AND DISCUSSION

1. What factors are involved in dating the birth of Jesus Christ? Explain how he could be born *B.C.*

2. In approximately what year did Christ begin his public ministry? Give the references to the important texts that bear upon this question and tell how each relates to it.

3. Which Gospel helps us know the length of Jesus' ministry, and how does it do that?

4. Discuss the views for the day of the week on which Jesus was crucified. Use Scripture in your discussion.

5. About what year was Jesus crucified?

6. Give the date and Scripture chapters for the death of Herod Agrippa I, the famine under Claudius, the proconsulship of Gallio, and Festus' coming as procurator of Judea.

7. Cite and explain the important Scripture passages that establish the chronology of Paul's conversion and ministry. Does Gal 2 fit better with Acts 11 or 15? When was the Jerusalem Council?

8. Construct a simple chart to show the correlation between Paul's missionary journeys and the epistles he wrote, with approximate dates for each.

IV.   FOR FURTHER READING AND RESEARCH

Andrews, Samuel James. *The Life of Our Lord Upon the Earth.* Grand Rapids: Zondervan, 1954. pp. 1-52.

Armstrong, William P. "Chronology of the New Testament." *The International Standard Bible Encyclopaedia.* Ed. J. Orr. Grand Rapids: Eerdmans, 1939. I, 644B-650.

Bruce, F. F., and F. F. Bruce. *Paul, Apostle of the Heart Set Free.* Carlisle, Cumbria, UK: Paternoster, 2000. 510 pp.

Caird, George B. "The Chronology of the Bible." *The Interpreter's Dictionary of the Bible.* Ed. G. A. Buttrick. Nashville: Abingdon, 1962. I, 599-607.

Finegan, Jack. *Handbook of Biblical Chronology: Principles of Time Reckoning in the Ancient World and Problems of Chronology in the Bible.* Rev. ed. Peabody, MA: Hendrickson, 1998. xxxviii + 426.

Hitchcock, F. R. Montgomery. "Dates." *Dictionary of Christ and the Gospels*. Ed. James Hastings. New York: Scribner's, 1906. I, 408-417.

Hoehner, Harold W. *Chronological Aspects of the Life of Christ*. Grand Rapids: Zondervan, 1977. 176 pp.

Ogg, George. *The Chronology of the Public Ministry of Jesus*. Cambridge [Eng.]: The University Press, 1940. viii + 339.

Ramsay, William Mitchell. *Pauline and Other Studies in Early Christian History*. Grand Rapids: Baker, 1970. xi + 415.

_____. *The Bearing of Recent Discovery on the Trustworthiness of the New Testament*. Grand Rapids: Baker, 1953. xvi + 427.

Robertson, A. T., and John Albert Broadus. *A Harmony of the Gospels*. New York: Harper & Brothers, 1950. xxxvii + 304.

Thompson, W. Ralph. "Chronology of the New Testament." *The Zondervan Pictorial Bible Encyclopedia*. Ed. M.C. Tenney. Grand Rapids: Zondervan, 1975. I, 816-829.

Turner, Cuthbert Hamilton. "Chronology of the New Testament." *Dictionary of the Bible*. Ed. James Hastings. Edinburgh: T. & T. Clark, 1908. I, 403-425.

9

NEW TESTAMENT BIBLICAL ARCHAEOLOGY

I. DEFINING BIBLICAL ARCHAEOLOGY

Archaeology is a relatively recent field of study. Prior to 1850, and even somewhat after that time, archaeology was more of a treasure hunt than a science. In fact, the father of modern archaeology, Sir Flinders Petrie, was not even born until 1853. His methodology, particularly his principle of *stratigraphy* (understanding the different layers or levels of an excavation), revolutionized the science of archaeology.

Archaeology is the science which uncovers and explains the past evidences of man's civilization. *Biblical archaeology* restricts itself to the periods, areas, and peoples covered in the Bible. New Testament biblical archaeology is concerned with these matters as they touch the New Testament records. The New Testament period stretches backward into the era that produced such persons as Mary and Joseph, Zachariah and Elizabeth, Caesar Augustus, Herod the Great, Gamaliel, and Nicodemus. It also reaches forward to the end of the first century A.D. when John wrote the

Apocalypse. The people's cultures to be explored include the Romans, Greeks, Galatians, Cretans, Jews, Samaritans, and many other smaller groups. The major countries where these remains are to be found include Israel, Jordan, Lebanon, Syria, Turkey, Greece, and Italy. Other countries visited by New Testament personalities would include Egypt (Matt 2:13-15; Acts 18:24), and Iraq (1 Peter 5:13).

II. THE VALUES OF BIBLICAL ARCHAEOLOGY

There are at least five distinct purposes or values for biblical archaeology. The knowledge gained can and should be put to such useful purposes as illumination, supplementation, confirmation, translation, and correction.

A. Illumination

Biblical archaeology frequently provides some general background for the history of the New Testament period by showing what the world was like. It illuminates our view of customs, clothing, material objects, coins, patterns of trade, travel, occupations, housing, government, religion and many other aspects of different cultures. This helps create the context for understanding the events of Scripture.

B. Supplementation

The Bible does not intend to, nor does it provide, a complete record of history. It is very selective, noting the important events about Israel, the Messiah, and salvation. Gallio, for

THE VALUES OF BIBLICAL ARCHAEOLOGY

1. *ILLUMINATION*

It provides some good general background for the history of the Bible, and creates the context for the events of Scripture. (Customs, clothing, material objects, religions, commerce, travel, occupations, etc.)

2. *SUPPLEMENTATION*

The Bible does not provide a *complete* record of history. It is very selective, noting the important events about Israel and salvation. (The story of Omri, for example, is mentioned in only 16 verses of the Bible, yet he was a very important person in the ancient world, and Israel was referred to as the House of Omri).

3. *CONFIRMATION*

W. R. Ramsay's doubts about Luke's accuracy vanished when he discovered at Delphi an inscription about Gallio being in Achaia when Paul was at Corinth.

4. *TRANSLATION*

Some biblical words occur in the text only once *(hapax legoumena), but are found elsewhere in archaeology. Semitic languages are very similar, and rare words, cognates, idioms, etc., found in other languages help us to properly translate and interpret the Bible.*

5. *CORRECTION*

Critic's ideas and charges that the Bible is of doubtful historicity have been substantially challenged. (See quotes from Free and Albright on p. 108).

example, is mentioned only briefly in Acts 18:12-17. Archaeology supplements this cursory biblical reference with information about his family. He was the brother of Seneca who was the tutor and chief advisor of Nero! Archaeology also tells us that he was proconsul of Achaia for *only* one year, and that the particular year was A.D. 51-52.

C. Confirmation

Sir William Ramsay (1851-1939) was an unbelieving skeptic who set out to prove Luke wrong historically. As an archaeologist himself, he found again and again that Luke's accuracy was overwhelmingly confirmed through his discoveries in Greece, Turkey and elsewhere. The historicity of Pilate was also confirmed when in 1967 a large Roman stone inscription was uncovered in Caesarea bearing most of his name--[PON]*TIUS PILATUS.*

D. Translation

Some biblical words occur in the New Testament text only once (*hapax legoumena*), but are found elsewhere in archaeology where their meanings become more apparent. This aids in translating passages where single-occurring words are found. In addition to rare words, idiomatic phrases and special syntactical usages found in the Koine Greek used in New Testament times are helpful. The Greek of the New Testament was called *Koine* (common), and was spread world-wide previously by Alexander the Great. It was the language of the common man and many papyri discoveries aid our translation process.

E. Correction

Although the interpretation of an archaeological find is sometimes disputed, many of the critics' ideas that the Bible is of doubtful historicity have been substantially challenged. False concepts and impressions have been corrected. Joseph P. Free, who headed the Dothan expedition in Israel for many years, and taught at Wheaton College, stated that archaeology "confirms countless passages which have been rejected by critics as unhistorical or contradictory to known facts."[1] W. F. Albright, the dean of American archaeologists and a Semitics professor at Johns Hopkins University, boldly claimed that "there can be no doubt that archaeology has confirmed the substantial historicity of Old Testament tradition."[2]

III. FOUR ESSENTIAL INGREDIENTS OF ARCHAEOLOGY

Four important factors govern the progress and output of modern archaeology. There always has been a crucial interplay between the four essential P's--the *People,* the *Plans,* the *Physical Objects,* and the *Purse.* Without people no expeditions would be possible, but apart from proper plans--a *modus operandi,* the mission's results would be of uncertain value. Naturally, without the physical objects to find there would be

---

[1]Joseph P. Free, *Archaeology and Bible History* (Wheaton: Scripture Press, 1964), p. 1.

[2]William Foxwell Albright, *Archaeology and the Religion of Israel* 4th ed. (Baltimore: Johns Hopkins, 1956), p. 176.

no point in going, but only the purse--adequate financing--makes it all happen.

A. The People

Many people are needed to combine efforts on a successful archaeological dig or project. There are many jobs to fill from that of surveyor and photographer to cook and dirt carrier. Professors contribute expert knowledge, students bring eager minds, and nationals fill many positions. It is a group effort and takes many willing participants.

B. The Plans

As with any project a plan is essential. How are the artifacts to be unearthed--by bulldozer or by toothbrush? A wrong decision could be costly. Usually an intricate grid system is laid out over a proposed dig and every important item found is systematically recorded with its original position on the grid duly noted, measured, and photographed. This is all part of methodology and defines how the operation will proceed. Brief notes about stratigraphy and pottery dating might be helpful at this point.

1.*Stratigraphy.* Sir Flinders Petrie was the first one to develop the seemingly obvious principle of stratigraphy. He asserted that ancient ruins, especially cities in the near east, were deposited layer by layer--the oldest being on the bottom, and the more recent materials being progressively toward the top. Many sites in Israel are composed of 20-25 distinct layers which indicate the many different occupations of that place. Some ruins contain Canaanite remains near the bottom, followed by Israelite, Greek,

Roman, and Byzantine civilizations and perhaps a crusader castle on top! Of course, many other cultures may have left their mark somewhere in between.

2. ***Pottery Dating.*** About 15 years ago I visited Israel for the first time. While touring the Rockefeller Museum I grew tired and sat down by a fountain. I met a young bearded American student in sandals sitting there engaged in a book. I inquired, and the book was for a class in *pottery* at the Hebrew University. I thought it must be something like the proverbial "Basket-Weaving I," but I was mistaken. I soon discovered that pottery was the *primary* means of dating all layers of a *tell* (a city composed of different occupational levels left in the shape of a large mound). Pottery is extremely useful for dating purposes for several reasons: (1) Pottery is amply found in the various layers--having been discarded as it became broken and having weathered the centuries. (2) Pottery styles and materials of composition changed with each culture and over time, making it easy to date a level by the distinctive pottery found there. An accurate knowledge of pottery is practically like having a chart with dates and the names of cultures printed on it. Petrie was also the first to suggest pottery as a means of dating the levels of a tell.

C.　The Physical Objects

Pottery is not the only physical object to be found in digs. City walls, streets, fountains, forums, and fortresses are uncovered, along with temples, tombs, catacombs, churches, statues and synagogues. These are examples of *monumental* remains. Smaller objects made by man, commonly called *artifacts,* include tools, weapons, crafts, arts, utensils, chariots and so forth. In addition, written *inscriptions* are found on wood, copper plates, stone, clay, coins, cylinders, papyrus, and skins. These are the physical objects that explain the people and their culture when properly interpreted.

D. The Purse

Apart from adequate financing, archaeology would not be able to proceed. The primary purse strings are held by schools, governments, museums, and philanthropic organizations and individuals. Any of these may sponsor or partially sponsor a project for obvious reasons. The primary costs often include the purchase of the site and the land around it, equipment for excavating, travel, housing and food for participants, local labor fees, dumping costs, and later publication costs.

IV. FAMOUS ARCHAEOLOGISTS

A number of men and women have made significant contributions to the field of archaeology, affecting both Old and New Testament studies. The following section lists just fifteen of the most well-known names with a brief word about the work of each.

1. *William F. Albright (1891-1971).* For thirty years W. F. Albright taught at Johns Hopkins University, wrote hundreds of books and articles, excavated at Bethel, Gibeah, and Petra, and is called the Dean of Biblical Archaeologists.

2. ***James Breasted (1865-1935).*** James Breasted was the greatest Egyptologist of his day and taught at the University of Chicago.

3. ***Jean F. Champollion (1790-1832).*** Champollion deciphered the Rosetta Stone in 1822 which opened up Egypt's hieroglyphic writing. The stone, discovered by Napoleon's army in Egypt in 1799, was written in Greek, Egyptian Demotic script, and in hieroglyphics.

4. ***John Garstang (1876-1956).*** John Garstang excavated in England, Egypt, Asia Minor, Syria, Sudan, and in Palestine--primarily at Jericho.

5. ***Nelson Glueck (1900-1971).*** Nelson Glueck conducted numerous ground surveys in trans-Jordan and was President of Hebrew Union College.

6. ***Kathleen Kenyon (1906-1978).*** Miss Kenyon was Director of the British School of Archaeology and dug up Jericho and Davidic Jerusalem.

7. ***Benjamin Mazar (1906-1995).*** As President of the Hebrew University and the Israel Exploration Society, Benjamin Mazar has been in charge of the Temple excavations in Jerusalem.

8. ***Sir Flinders Petrie (1853-1942).*** The father of modern archaeology, Sir Flinders Petrie wrote over 100 books and discovered pottery dating and the layer system in tells.

9. ***James Pritchard (1909-1997).*** James Pritchard, as a professor at the University of Pennsylvania, excavated extensively in Palestine and edited *Ancient Near Eastern Texts (ANET)*.

10. ***Sir William Ramsay (1851-1939).*** Sir William Ramsay of the University of Aberdeen

was the greatest New Testament archaeologist, specializing in Asia Minor and sites relating to Paul.

11. **Henry C. Rawlinson (1810-1895).** While with the British army in Persia, Henry Rawlinson copied and decoded the Behistun Stone of Darius I.

12. **Roland de Vaux (1903-1971).** As a French leader in Palestinian archaeology, and head of the Ecole Biblique in Jerusalem, Roland de Vaux, had a part in the Dead Sea scrolls expeditions, and in work at Bethlehem and Hebron.

13. **Leonard Woolley (1880-1960).** British archaeologist Leonard Woolley dug up Ur of the Chaldees, Carchemish, Amarna, and Alalakh.

14. **G. Ernest Wright (1909-1974).** G. Ernest Wright was President of the American Society of Oriental Research, founder of *Biblical Archaeologist,* and dug at Gezer and Shechem.

15. **Yigael Yadin (1917-1984).** Yigael Yadin, an Israeli, directed digs as Hazor, Masada, Megiddo, and the Judean desert. He discovered the Bar Kochba letters.

V. FOR REVIEW AND DISCUSSION

1. Define as precisely as possible what New Testament biblical archaeology is. With what periods of time, peoples, and countries is it concerned?

2. List and describe the five principle values or purposes of biblical archaeology.

3. Discuss the four essential ingredients of archaeology. What are the factors that constitute each of these essentials?

4. Be able to list about ten important archaeologists, noting the contribution(s), and/or position in life of each.

VI.   FOR FURTHER READING AND RESEARCH

Blaiklock, E. M., and R. K. Harrison, eds. *The New International Dictionary of Biblical Archaeology.* Grand Rapids: Zondervan, 1983. xxvii + 485.

Gower, Ralph. *The New Manners & Customs of Bible Times.* Chicago: Moody Press, 2005. 352 pp.

Hoerth, Alfred J., and John McRay. *Bible Archaeology.* Grand Rapids: Baker, 2005. 288 pp.

Hoffmeier, James Karl, and Alan R. Millard, eds. *The Future of Biblical Archaeology.* Grand Rapids: Eerdmans, 2004. xviii + 385.

Ramsay, William Mitchell. *St. Paul the Traveller and the Roman Citizen.* London: Hodder and Stoughton, 1897. xxviii + 402.

_____. *The Bearing of Recent Discovery on the Trustworthiness of the New Testament.* Grand Rapids: Baker; reprinted 1953. xiv + 427.

_____. *The Cities of St. Paul.* London: Hodder and Stoughton, 1907. xvi + 452.

Schoville, Keith N. *Biblical Archaeology in Focus.* Grand Rapids: Baker, 1978. 511 pp.

Vos, Howard Frederic. *Nelson's New Illustrated Bible Manners & Customs.* Nashville: Thomas Nelson, 1999. viii + 661.

Yamauchi, Edwin M. *The Archaeology of New Testament Cities in Western Asia Minor.* Grand Rapids: Baker, 1980. 180 pp.

PART TWO

THE CANON
AND TEXT

10

THE INSPIRATION AND ORIGIN OF THE NEW TESTAMENT BOOKS

I. THE INSPIRATION OF THE NEW TESTAMENT

A. A Word of Introduction

Although inspiration is a subject more germane to the theological area of bibliology, it is still quite appropriate to discuss it briefly in an introduction to the New Testament. If the Bible is not really the Word of God, then one needs to be told that before he gets too far along.

I am reminded of an encounter I had during my first year as a seminary professor in Minneapolis. A married student had been saved in Los Angeles through a campus ministry and felt called to serve God as a pastor. His own pastor recommended their denominational seminary in St. Paul. The student was dismayed when he discovered that the school and its professors were Neo-Orthodox, or worse, and believed the Bible to be full of errors. The poor dismayed student was ready to give up-- for if that was the kind of Bible he had to declare, then he would rather not proclaim it. Fortunately, two weeks later God led him to our seminary which believed and taught the Word of God, and he has been serving God in the ministry now for many years.

Is the Bible inspired or not? We must know. It cannot be an open question. It is not something I wish to debate. I want the matter settled with certainty. Yet is it possible to really know, or is it only a matter of belief and trust? One's faith is only as good as the object in which it is placed. Faith in the Word of God is as secure as the God who backs it up!

B. The Vocabulary of Inspiration

A host of terminology, some new and perhaps confusing, accompanies the debate over inspiration. Because of the fine nuances of language, the skill with which some use weasel-words, and the breadth of the controversy across many churches and denominations, one needs to know and define the vocabulary and terminology of inspiration.

1. *Inerrant.* Inerrant means without error. No mistakes of any kind whatever are possible in something that is inerrant. An inerrant Bible contains nothing that is untrue, false or incorrect, and all it speaks about is without error--even in matters of science, history, geography, and so forth.

2. *Inspired.* The English word inspired comes from the Latin *inspiro* which means to breathe upon or into. We are told that "all Scripture is given by inspiration of God" (2 Tim 3:16). The phrase "given by inspiration of God" is a translation of the single Greek word *theopneustos,* which means literally "God-breathed." The

THE DOCTRINE OF INSPIRATION

The *PRODUCT* of Inspiration--2 TIM 3:16

πᾶσα γραφὴ θεόπνευστος = every writing (Scripture)
is God-breathed.

The *PROCESS* of Inspiration--2 PET 1:21

KJV--*"moved* by the Holy Ghost"
Douay, ASV, RSV, NASB, NKJV--*"carried along* by the Holy Spirit"
Knox, Moffatt--*"carried away* by the Holy Spirit"
Williams--*"led* by the Holy Spirit"
TEV--*"under the control* of the Holy Spirit"

A *DEFINITION* of Inspiration

The best definition of inspiration I have ever seen comes from A. A. Hodge in *The Confession of Faith, pp. 33-34.*

"The books of Scripture were written by the instrumentality of men, and the national and personal peculiarities of their authors have been evidently as freely expressed in their writing, and their natural faculties, intellectual and moral, as freely exercised in their production, as those of the authors of any other writings. Nevertheless these books are, one and all, in thought and verbal expression, in substance and form, wholly the Word of God, conveying with absolute accuracy and divine authority all that God meant them to convey, without any human additions or admixtures. This was accomplished by a supernatural influence of the Spirit of God acting upon the spirits of the sacred writers, called 'inspiration;' which accompanied them uniformly in what they wrote; and which, without violating the free operation of their faculties, yet directed them in all they wrote, and secured the infallible expression of it in words. The nature of this divine influence we, of course, can no more understand than we can in the case of any other miracle. But the effects are plain and certain--viz., that all written under it is the very Word of God, of infallible truth, and of divine authority; and this infallibility and authority attach as well to the verbal expression in which the revelation is conveyed as to the matter of the revelation itself."

Used by Permission. Banner of Truth. Box 621, Carlisle, PA 17013.

Scriptures--the actual writings themselves--have the quality of being God-breathed. They come directly from God who breathes into, through, and out of them. That is *why* they are inerrant. They are not merely the words nor the works of men. The finished product, the *graphe,* the writing itself, is God-breathed and as a result is inerrant.

3. **Verbal.** From the Latin *verbum,* word, comes the corresponding English term--verbal. Verbal inspiration is a declaration that each and every word (even the very spelling of each word) is totally from God.

4. **Plenary.** Plenary, from the Latin *plenus,* means full, complete, and entire. Plenary inspiration means that all parts--beginning, middle, and end; prose and poetry; history and apocalypse; parable and prophecy; genealogy or any other literary genre--are all fully and completely God-breathed.

5. **Credal Statements.** Doctrinal statements are necessary and useful in preserving a clear understanding of what a person or a group believes. But all too frequently people's views change. Without bothering to (or daring to) change their doctrinal statements, some simply incorporate a new understanding into the old phrases. That is why it is best to clearly *define* inspiration, rather than simply to *affirm* it though void of any reality. Definitions are most helpful when they are both positive and negative. An example follows:

The Bible, all sixty-six books, were written under the inspiration of God. As such, every book was verbally and plenarily God-breathed, and is inerrant in all matters it speaks to--including history, science, geography, or any other subject. No errors of any kind were involved in God's transmission of His Word to those who wrote it down. The finished product was perfect and conveyed God's message with absolute accuracy.

C. The Place of Presuppositions

The Bible presupposes and claims its own inspiration. It may be logical to reason that if God were intelligent and personal we might expect Him to communicate with us. And indeed there are standard "proofs" of the Bible's worth and truth based on its (1)fulfilled prophecy, (2) unity, (3) contents, and (4) influence.

But, the claim that the Scriptures make for themselves is the important matter. The Holy Spirit inspired the Word of God (2 Peter 1:19-21), and it is His powerful Word itself which He will use to convince men of that truth. No amount of logic, rationalism, or persuasion can ever equal the convicting power of God's Word.

In Isa 55:11 God states "My word . . . shall not return to Me void, But it shall accomplish what I please." John 16:7-11 declare that part of the work of the Holy Spirit is to convict and convince the world of sin, righteousness, and judgment. Conviction can be either objective or subjective. *Objectively,* the work has been accomplished--man stands convicted. But *subjectively,* man can inwardly refuse to admit what he knows to be true. It is a matter of the will to trust God and to believe His Holy Word.

D. The Use of Proof Texts

The trouble with proof texts is that they can be taken out of context. A person could actually string together verses from the Bible which say that Judas Iscariot "went and hanged himself"

(Matt 27:5); "Go and do likewise" (Luke 10:37); and "What you do, do quickly" (John 13:27). However, some individual verses more than others zero in on particular subjects and concisely express whatever the truth might be. Most verses are clear and plain in their meaning and are meant for our "doctrine, for reproof, for correction, for instruction in righteousness" (2 Tim 3:16). There are several outstanding texts that bear upon the doctrine of inspiration.

1. **2 Tim 3:16 and 2 Peter 1:21.** Perhaps the two most often quoted verses on the doctrine of inspiration are 2 Tim 3:16 and 2 Peter 1:21. One speaks of the *product* of inspiration as being God-breathed (2 Tim 3:16), while the other attributes the *process* to the direct agency of the Holy Spirit (2 Peter 1:21). God actively insured that the words long ago written in Hebrew and in Greek were perfect and without error (product). He also actively and supernaturally guided the writers while they wrote to insure no mistakes (process). These two texts are very powerful statements.

2. **Matt 5:18 and John 10:35.** Two additional texts contain statements by Christ Himself. Matt 5:18 declares that "one jot or one tittle will by no means pass from the law till all is fulfilled." This verse probably does not argue for some miraculous preservation of a manuscript or even the safeguarding of the copying process. Rather, it seems to verify the certainty of the future fulfillment of all God's promises. Nothing written or promised by God will ever fail to be accomplished.

John 10:35, on the other hand, speaks more directly of inspiration where Jesus said, "and the Scripture cannot be broken." Jesus declared that the *graphe,* the writing itself, the very words used in Psa 82:6 were of the utmost authority. Even a tiny verse was of unchanging infallibility. The argument from this says that if that were so for such a minor verse in Psalms, then it must be true also for the whole of Scripture. The words of Scripture cannot be set aside, done away with, or abolished. They speak with a perpetually binding force.

3. *1 Thess 2:13 and 1 Cor 14:37.* Paul and the other Apostles knew that they spoke for God, receiving direct revelation as they proclaimed Christ and laid the foundation of the church (Eph 2:20). Twice Paul clearly asserted that his messages and *words* were the very words of God. In 1 Thess 2:13 Paul reminded the believers in Thessalonica "when you received the word of God which you heard from us, you welcomed it not as the word of men, but as it is in truth, the word of God." Again, to the Corinthians Paul exhorted all spiritual believers to "acknowledge that the things which I write to you are the commandments of the Lord" (1 Cor 14:37). Paul claimed to *speak* and *write* the very words of God-- which indeed he did.

4. *1 Tim 5:18 and 2 Peter 3:15-16.* Finally, two additional texts speak of New Testament inspiration. In 1 Tim 5:18, Paul quotes from two separate passages after introducing them with the phrase "For the Scripture says." One of these "Scripture" passages is none other than six words of Jesus quoted *verbatim* from Luke 10:7. The Gospel of Luke was published about five years before Paul wrote 1 Tim, and not one vowel or syllable is missing. Paul regarded Luke as Scripture.

Then again, Peter regarded Paul's writings as Scripture. 2 Peter 3:15-16 clearly imply this where

Peter accuses the untaught of twisting Paul's words "in all his epistles ... as they do also the rest of the Scriptures." The New Testament is totally inspired, inerrant, and infallible from beginning to end.

II.   THE ORIGIN OF THE NEW TESTAMENT BOOKS

The purpose of the New Testament is to provide an authoritative and infallible record of the person and work of the Lord Jesus Christ, the founding and early progress of the church, God's expectations for believers, and Christ's future coming and attendant events. The actual writings were historically conditioned--that is, they arose as there was a human need for the writing. This concept of the origin of the New Testament books is briefly outlined below.

A.   The Gospels

The earliest of the four Gospels was probably Matt. The story about Christ circulated in Palestine and among the Jews for years before it ever went to the Gentiles. Matt no doubt early fulfilled the need among *the Jews* for an official account of Jesus' life and ministry. But later in the early A.D. 50's the missionary journeys carried Paul and Silas into Greece. Luke, a Gospel tailored to the *Greek* frame of reference, was produced about A.D. 58-60 while Paul was imprisoned in Caesarea. Luke would have had ample time to personally research and interview witnesses during these two years with Paul in Palestine. Later, after Paul's Roman detention, a written story of Christ could be prepared and suited for the *Roman* mind. That was Mark's Gospel, written perhaps about A.D. 67. John came many years later as a conscious supplement of the three previous works, and as a spiritual Gospel addressed to *all mankind* to encourage belief in Christ (John 20:30-31).

B. The Epistles

The New Testament contains 21 epistles written by a total of five or six persons--Paul (13), John (3), Peter (2), James (1), Jude (1), and Hebrews. The latter two individuals (James and Jude), were the sons of Mary and Joseph, and were Jesus' brothers (Mark 6:3; Gal 1:19; Jude 1).

Some of the earliest of all the epistles grew out of questions and problems that arose in Thessalonica on Paul's second missionary journey (A.D. 50-52). Gal was hastily written because a Judaizing heresy needed to be dealt with immediately (perhaps A.D. 49). Other epistles were penned to meet personal needs, as Philem, or to inform and thank for a gift, as Phil. 1 Peter went to churches in five Roman provinces (1:1), and was meant to encourage during a time of suffering and persecution. 2 Peter and Jude served as warnings and exhortations, as largely did Heb. Each epistle came out of historical conditions that called it forth.

C. The Acts

The Gospel story ends in Palestine with Christ's ascension, while the epistles depict churches and believers struggling in far away places with heretofore unmentioned leaders (Paul, Barnabas, Silas, Apollos, Aquila, Priscilla and others). Acts was needed to bridge the gap and explain the origin and history of the early church.

Luke had the opportunity to do this while with Paul in Rome between A.D. 60-62. He apparently published the Acts at the end of those two years in Rome (Acts 28:30) since that is the extent of the history recounted.

D. The Apocalypse

The Apocalypse appears in last place among the canonical books--presumably for two reasons: (1) it was the final book to be written; and (2) it serves as the climax and consummation of the entire Word of God. It was penned just before the end of the first century A.D.

III. THE LOCATION OF THE NEW TESTAMENT MANUSCRIPTS

The original documents of the New Testament were deposited into the hands of various churches and individuals throughout the eastern Mediterranean area--particularly in those portions adjoining its northern shores. *Asia Minor,* present-day Turkey, probably received no fewer than thirteen of the original manuscripts of the New Testament including Gal, Eph, Col, Philem, 1 and 2 Tim, 1 and 2 Peter, 1-3 John, John's Gospel, and Rev. *Greece* presumably was the recipient of seven New Testament works--1 and 2 Thess, 1 and 2 Cor, Phil, Luke and Acts, while *Italy* no doubt received Rom and Mark. *Palestine* at least had the manuscript of Matt, and Crete possessed Titus. The original destination of Heb, James, and Jude is perhaps uncertain. From all we can tell, Egypt (Alexandria) received *no* firsthand manuscripts.

The *initial* resting place of each New

Testament manuscript may have a much larger bearing on the matter of textual criticism than many critical scholars have admitted. The first generation of *copies* would have sprung forth and multiplied in the same areas as their original destination. That may be the simplest and best explanation for the preponderance of manuscripts, commonly called the Majority Text, which many believe came from Asia Minor and Greece. A fairly uniform text is found in the Majority family as opposed to the divergent texts that may come from Egypt. The handful of divergent manuscripts may represent an emasculated text that developed away from the preponderance of manuscripts that could have provided the necessary corrections for scribal errors, omissions, and emendations.

IV   FOR REVIEW AND DISCUSSION

1.   Carefully discuss the meaning of the terms *theopneustos,* inerrant, inspired, verbal, and plenary as they apply to the doctrine of inspiration.

2.   Is it important to have a written credal statement about inspiration? How and when should such statements be updated and/or strengthened?

3.   Does the doctrine of inspiration rest upon proof or presupposition? Are the statements in the Bible about inspiration enough, or must one always "prove" the Bible's inerrancy to the spiritually lost? Do you think one could prove inerrancy to a critic's full satisfaction? Why, or why not?

4.   What is the essential teaching and/or meaning of 2 Tim 3:16, 2 Peter 1:21, Matt 5:18,

John 10:35, 1 Thess 2:13, 1 Cor 14:37, 1 Tim 5:18,
and 2 Peter 3:15-16. How does each of these texts
bear on the matter of the inspiration of the Bible?
5.   What is the ruling principle regarding the
origin of the New Testament books? Discuss how
the Gospels, Epistles, Acts, and Apocalypse came
into being.
6.   What might the *place of origin* of each of the
twenty-seven New Testament books have to do
with the types of text available today, *i.e.* majority
vs. critical? Where did the various books actually
reside? Would the original type of text presumably
have dominated in these areas? Why, or why not?

V.   FOR FURTHER READING AND RESEARCH

Boice, James Montgomery. Ed. *The Foundation of Biblical Authority.* Grand Rapids: Zondervan, 1978.   172 pp.

Gaussen, Louis. *Theopneustia.* Trans. David Scott. Chicago: Moody, n.d.   xxii + 365.

Geisler, Norman L. Ed. *Inerrancy.* Grand Rapids: Zondervan, 1979.   x + 516.

Harris, R. Laird. *Inspiration and Canonicity of the Bible.* Grand Rapids: Zondervan, 1957.   316 pp.

Hodge, Archibald Alexander. *The Confession of Faith.* London: Banner of Truth; reprinted, 1961.   pp. 25-45.

Lightner, Robert P. *The Saviour and the Scriptures.* Grand Rapids: Baker, 1966   vi + 178.

Warfield, Benjamin Breckinridge. *The Inspiration and Authority of the Bible.* Ed. Samuel G. Craig. Philadelphia: Presbyterian and Reformed, 1948.

Young, Edward J. *Thy Word Is Truth.* Grand Rapids: Eerdmans, 1957.   287 pp.

11

THE FORMATION OF THE NEW TESTAMENT CANON

I. WHAT IS CANONIZATION?

The word canon refers to the thirty-nine Old Testament and the twenty-seven New Testament books which came to be accepted as the genuinely inspired and authoritative written Word of God. Originally, in Greek, the word canon meant a straight rod, then it was applied to that which tested straightness (as a ruler), and finally to that which was accepted as meeting a particular standard (the rule). Thus, the canonical Scriptures are those that meet the tests of what Scripture is.

The process by which this determination was made is called canonization. It should be seen as a *process* rather than as an act or a vote by some ecclesiastical council. It was also a slow process, a gradual growing concensus of opinion about the books of the New Testament. There were questions and doubts about some of the books, but these were eventually settled satisfactorily.

II. THE PROCESS OF CANONIZATION

A. Early Public Reading and Circulation

As the books of the New Testament were written and sent to various churches and individuals, they were read publicly in the churches. 1 Thess 5:27 says, "I charge you by the Lord that this epistle be read to all the holy brethren." A similar charge is found in 1 Tim 4:13 "give attention to reading," and in Col 4:16 which mentions both the reading of Col as well as the reading of an epistle from the nearby church at Laodicea. Rev 1:3 speaks of the common practice of reading the Word in the churches, and 2 Peter 3:15-16 declare Paul's writings to be a collection of Scripture. Again, 1 Tim 5:18 classifies Luke as Scripture also.

As the writings circulated and copies were made, especially in the Asia Minor-Greece region, where most of the books originated, more and more churches and believers became familiar with the authoritative New Testament writings. However, to complicate matters somewhat, additional books were later composed and circulated after the end of the apostolic age. Some of these books--Hermas, Barnabas, the Didache, and 1 Clement--gained a measure of respect and recognition as ecclesiastical writings, and caused some confusion in places about which books were to be regarded as canonical. A further amount of uncertainty was created by doubts over some of the regular canonical books--for reasons discussed under III. below.

B. New Testament Use from A.D. 100-200

How much of the New Testament did some of the early Christian leaders have, use, and accept as "canonical"? The year A.D. 200 is still early and formative in terms of church history and the history of the canon. Most writers prior to that time wrote only sparingly, mentioning a number of New Testament books, but perhaps not having occasion to quote from all of them. But three men stand out as ecclesiastical giants at the end of the second century A.D. Numerous works remain from their pens. These three represent different areas of the church, so their united testimony is even stronger than their single voices. Clement was a theologian and teacher in Alexandria (Egypt); Tertullian was a lawyer in Carthage (North Africa); and Irenaeus was a bishop in Lyons (Gaul or France).

1. *Clement of Alexandria.* The works of Clement of Alexandria that are extant fill a good-sized volume. He fought heresies and dealt with the issues of the day. There was not one book of the New Testament that he did not accept, but he apparently had no occasion to quote from or comment on James, 2 Peter, and 3 John. Thus Clement essentially held the same New Testament as believers do today.

2. *Tertullian of Carthage.* Tertullian wrote primarily in Latin and his extensive works are still available today in English translations (*The Ante-Nicene Fathers*). He apparently received all of our twenty-seven books with the exception of Heb which he thought was authored by Barnabas, although he also did not have occasion to cite James, 2 Peter, and 2 and 3 John. Frequently, however, 2 and 3 John would be bound with 1

John, so that a reference to it was tantamount to indicating possession of the others as well.

3. *Irenaeus of Lyons.* Irenaeus was a disciple of Polycarp in Smyrna, and Polycarp was in turn a disciple of the Apostle John, so his testimony is significant. He cites from or alludes to the four Gospels, Acts, all of Paul's epistles except the short book of Philem, plus 1 Peter, 1 John, and Rev. He may have been familiar with the other books as well (Heb and several of the general epistles), but he did not mention them in either a good or bad context.

4. *Other Early Writers.* The writings of Clement of Rome, Ignatius, Justin Martyr, Polycarp, Papias, Melito, Theophilus, Athenagoras, and Tatian are not as full as those of "The Big Three" listed above. Yet as a group, even these earlier writers freely cite from nearly every New Testament book. An early list of books, called the Muratorian Fragment (A.D. 170), mentions each of the twenty-seven canonical books except Heb, James and 1 and 2 Peter. Melito also quotes or alludes to all except four--James, Jude, and 2 and 3 John. Again, for different reasons, some writers expressed rejection of a book now and then. Tatian may not have accepted 1 Tim. Marcion, a Gnostic heretic, rejected all but some of Luke and Paul's first ten epistles.

C. New Testament Use from A.D. 200-400

During the two centuries from A.D. 200-400 many writers of stature left record of their use of the New Testament books. In Alexandria, Origen (died A.D. 253), distinguished between the accepted books and those about which there was

THE N. T. CANON DURING THE FIRST FOUR CENTURIES

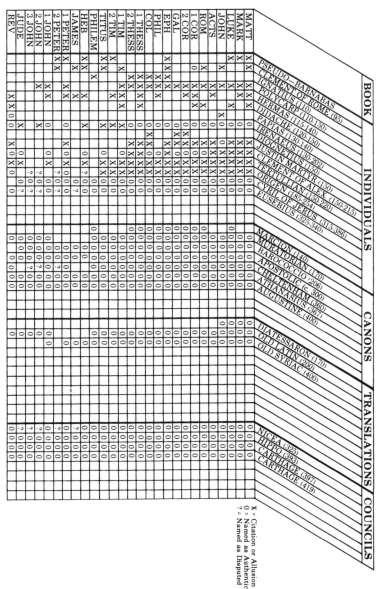

X = Citation or Allusion
0 = Named as Authentic
? = Named as Disputed

still some debate. Nevertheless, he apparently accepted all 27 books, plus a couple extras-- Hermas and the Didache. Athanasius, also of Alexandria (died 373), actually used the word canon to designate the 27 books of the New Testament. Cyril of Jerusalem (died 386), mentions the church's acceptance of each of the 27 books with the single exception of Rev.

Jerome (died 420), the translator of the Latin Vulgate, included only our 27 books, and Augustine of Hippo (died 430) seems to have accepted all of the canonical books even though he may have given more weight to some than to others. Lucian of Antioch (died 312) did not include 2 Peter, 2 and 3 John, Jude, and Rev, while Gregory Nazianzus (died 390) rejected only Rev. Two brothers, Basil the Great (died 379) and Gregory of Nyssa (died 400), both of Cappadocia, rejected none of the 27 books.

Several church councils confirmed what was the general concensus of opinion in the church. The Third Council of Carthage in A.D. 397 spoke of the canon and listed precisely the 27 books accepted today. That was the very first council to address the subject of the canon, yet by that time opinion had matured to such a degree that little opposition persisted beyond A.D. 400.

II. THE RULING PRINCIPLES OF CANONIZATION

A number of important considerations seem to have been factors in the process of canonization. Why the twenty-seven books of our canon were eventually accepted seems to have been based on the very natural application of perhaps four principles.

A. Apostolic Authorship

The foremost ruling principle of the canonization process seems to have been that of apostolic authorship. Jesus spoke from God and was attested by John the Baptist (John 5:32-35), His miracles (John 5:36; Heb 2:4), God the Father (John 5:37), and the Scriptures themselves (John 5:39). His authority to speak from God was passed along to the Apostles (John 15:26-27; 16:13; 20:21), and their ministry was authenticated by divine works as well (Acts 2:43; 4:30; 5:12; 6:8; 14:3).

Thus, when an Apostle spoke, or wrote in the name of the Lord, his message was considered authoritative and accepted as the Word of God. They did not need to hold a council or vote on it at the next business meeting. Of the Gospel writers, two were Apostles and the other two were closely guided by the Apostles Peter and Paul. Paul's thirteen epistles were accepted because he was an Apostle. Questions were voiced in some quarters about James, Jude, John "the elder" (2 John 1; 3 John 1), and Heb because of the uncertainty of authorship.

B. Church Testimony and Use

The churches of Thessalonica, Philippi, Corinth, Rome, Colossae, and many others which received original apostolic letters could testify of that fact. Such continued testimony and their usage of these letters was no doubt a powerful witness to the genuineness and authority of those books. In time this initial testimony would spread abroad together with the usage of that particular New Testament book. Eventually, the opinion of the church would be unanimous and universal.

C. Doctrinal Reliability

The contents of each book had to evidence a doctrinal soundness and reliability. The prophet Isaiah declared that the revelation of a true prophet must conform to the law and the prophets, *i.e.,* previous revelation. 1 Clement disclaims inspiration, and Hermas' visions lack a certain credibility. Apocryphal books and heretical writings displayed gross inconsistencies from the teaching of the Old Testament, the words of Christ, and the other standard apostolic teaching and writings. Those books that may have seemed hard to judge by this criterion were eventually either attested as true or else set aside.

D. Inspiration

A fourth test that could be applied to some, but not all books was whether the writing claimed to be inspired. Many did not have occasion to speak in those terms but others did--especially some of Paul's works. We have already mentioned 1 Cor 14:37 and 1 Thess 2:13 which make such claims. But it should also be noted that in each case Paul challenges the Christians to recognize or acknowledge that the words he spoke and wrote were indeed inspired! There was an obligation on the part of Spirit-filled believers to perceive the spiritual contents and inspiration of the Word of God. That is because as Paul declared, it is "the word of God, which also effectively works in you who believe" (1 Thess 2:13).

A note of caution is in order at this point. Mormons and other cults claim to have new "apostles" who can receive and write Scripture, and they call upon the uninitiated to "read and recognize" it as from God. However, the outstanding point of difference is that their writings do not and cannot pass the scrutiny of points B and C above. The church universally *rejects* their claims, and their works fall under the curse of Gal 1:6 because they bring in a "different gospel" which does indeed "pervert the gospel of Christ" (Gal 1:7).

III. THE ANTILEGOMENA

Before there was complete universal agreement on the twenty-seven canonical New Testament books, twenty were accepted, while seven were sometimes questioned and/or rejected in some places. The reasons for the questions are reviewed at this point. The twenty accepted books were called the *homolegomena* (speak the same things about), and the seven questioned works were termed the *antilegomena* (the spoken against ones).

A. Hebrews

The authorship of the Book of Heb is uncertain. Some feel it was Paul, or Apollos, or Barnabas. Others suggest Clement, Aquila, Priscilla, Silas, or Luke. The author does not give his name, as Paul does in his thirteen recognized epistles, but the writer *is* known to his audience. He mentions that Timothy is in prison, but if and when Timothy is released, the writer will visit his readers with Timothy. This uncertainty clouded the full acceptance of Heb.

B. James

There are four men named James in the New Testament--James the son of Zebedee; James the

Less; James the father of Judas; and James the brother of Jesus Christ. Uncertainty about this authorship, and perhaps whether it was apostolic was a major question. Other issues related to the contents of the book (no particularly distinguishing Christian doctrine, or the faith vs. works question), and to it being addressed to "the twelve tribes which are scattered abroad" (James 1:1).

C. 2 Peter

The Epistle of 2 Peter differs somewhat in vocabulary and style from 1 Peter. Thus, some may have thought it to be a forgery. But would a forger risk discovery by departing so much from his model (1 Peter)? 1 Peter 5:12 says "by Silvanus . . . I have written to you," indicating an intermediate agency. Silvanus (Silas) may have been Peter's amanuensis, or scribe, for the *first* letter, possibly working with Peter on its composition, while Peter may not have had such help with his *second* epistle. Still, both letters claim to be the work of Peter in their introductions.

D. 2 and 3 John

The one chapter books of 2 and 3 John were sometimes omitted from lists of the New Testament books. One reason may have been that they were thought to be included with 1 John and did not need separate mentioning. However, the precise authorship of these tiny books was perhaps uncertain to some. The author calls himself "the elder." Certainly John the Apostle was an elder. But since these works are brief, personal, and relatively unimportant as far as their contents are concerned when compared, for example, with Rom, Gal, or 1 Cor, they were cited with far less frequency.

E. Jude

The short book of Jude was questioned for at least two reasons. First, who was Jude? The answer is that he was the son of Mary and Joseph, the brother of Jesus. As such he was an associate of the Apostles (Acts 1:14). Secondly, the reference to Enoch was thought by some to be an allusion to the pseudepigraphous work that bears his name. It need not be, but even if it is--any use Jude would make of Enoch would be wholly true and inspired, while Enoch itself is not.

F. Revelation

The Book of Rev was accepted early and was only later questioned, primarily as a result of Dionysius who argued in the fourth century that it differed too much from John's Gospel. It is true that Rev is an anomaly in many aspects of syntax and grammar, but it is also a unique book as far as New Testament literary genres are concerned. It is definitely apocalyptic vision-type literature, and for this reason some would doubt its propriety as part of the canon. Nevertheless, it is the fitting climax and consummation of the entire Word of God and was rightfully accepted as truly from its claimed author, John the Apostle (Rev 1:1, 4, 9; 21:2; 22:8).

IV. FACTORS WHICH HASTENED CANONIZATION

Several factors may have spurred the church into greater action in deciding which books were canonical and which deserved no place in the Scriptures. **(1)** Marcion, the Gnostic heretic, discarded all books except Luke and the first ten of Paul's epistles. This attempt to decrease the number of accepted books no doubt caused concern on the part of those who knew of the other sixteen books. The result was that Marcion was discredited and the New Testament survived his vicious attacks.

(2) On the other hand, some leaders looked with favor on *more* than the twenty-seven canonical books. What of Hermas, Clement, Barnabas, and the Didache (Teaching of the Twelve)? Some of these books were even copied into the giant codex manuscripts that contained the entire Bible. Discussion was quickened because of the existence of these extra-canonical books. Eventually they were judged to be good ecclesiastical literature, but *not* Scripture.

(3) A third development that may have hastened the selection process was the persecution by the Emperor Diocletian (A.D. 303). His edicts caused the destruction of as many Christian Scriptures as could be located. Christians had to decide for which books they might be willing to die. Hermas, Barnabas, Clement, and the Didache were not among them.

V. FOR REVIEW AND DISCUSSION

1.   What are the meanings of the word "canon," and what is canonization as applied to the Scriptures?
2.   Explain the *process* of canonization.
3.   Name the Big Three in church history who lived around A.D. 200. What contribution did each make regarding the canon?

4. List a number of early and later church fathers who bore witness to the books of the New Testament. Which ones were outstanding witnesses and how would you use their testimony in discussing the question of canonicity?

5. List and define the primary ruling principles of canonization. Discuss the strengths and weaknesses of each point.

6. Should any other "books," modern-day or otherwise, be considered Scripture besides the regular twenty-seven New Testament books? Why, or why not?

7. Distinguish between *homolegomena* and *antilegomena*. Why was each of the seven antilegomena books questioned?

8. Discuss the factors that may have hastened the process of canonization. Can you think of any other points that may have contributed to the process?

VI. FOR FURTHER READING AND RESEARCH

Abbot, Ezra. "The Canon of Scripture." *Smith's Dictionary of the Bible*. Ed. H. B. Hackett. Grand Rapids: Baker; reprinted, 1971. I, 356-376.

Allert, Craig D. *A High View of Scripture? The Authority of the Bible and the Formation of the New Testament Canon*. Grand Rapids: Baker Academic, 2007. 203 pp.

Beare, Frank W. "Canon of the New Testament." *The Interpreter's Dictionary of the Bible*. Ed. G. A. Buttrick. Nashville: Abingdon, 1962. I, 520-532

Borland, James A. "The Preservation of the New Testament Text: A Common Sense Approach," *The Master's Seminary Journal*, 10/1, Spring, 1999.

Brown, Raymond Edward. *An Introduction to the New Testament*. New York: Doubleday, 1997.

Carson, D. A. and Douglas J. Moo. *An Introduction to the New Testament.* Grand Rapids: Zondervan, 2005.

Gregory, Caspar Rene. *Canon and Text of the New Testament.* New York: Scribner's, 1907. viii + 539.

Guthrie, Donald. "The Canon of the New Testament." *The Zondervan Pictorial Encyclopedia of the Bible.* Ed. M. C. Tenney. Grand Rapids: Zondervan, 1975. I, 731-745.

Harris, R. Laird. *Inspiration and Canonicity of the Bible.* Grand Rapids: Zondervan, 1957. pp. 199-282.

Lea, Thomas D. and David Alan Black. *The New Testament: Its Background and Message.* Nashville: Broadman and Holman, 2003.

Metzger, Bruce Manning. *The Canon of the New Testament: Its Origin, Development and Significance.* New York: Oxford University Press, 1987.

Souter, Alexander. *The Canon and Text of the New Testament.* London: Duckworth, 1913. x + 254.

Thiessen, Henry Clarence. *Introduction to the New Testament.* Grand Rapids: Eerdmans, 1943. pp. 3-30.

Walls, Andrew F. "The Canon of the New Testament." *The Expositor's Bible Commentary.* Ed. F. E. Gaebelein. Grand Rapids: Zondervan, 1979. I, 631-643.

12

THE
TEXTUAL CRITICISM
OF THE
NEW TESTAMENT

I.   INTRODUCTION TO TEXTUAL CRITICISM

A.   What Textual Criticism Is

Textual criticism is sometimes referred to as *lower criticism*, not because it is inferior to higher criticism (date, authorship, genuineness, purpose, recipients), but because it is foundational to further study. Textual criticism is the science which seeks to discover the original text by comparing the various manuscript copies. There are more than 5,750 Greek manuscripts available. These include nearly 120 **papyri** copies, about 325 **uncials** (written in Greek capital letters), nearly 2,900 **miniscules** (written in a Greek cursive script), and about 2,450 **lectionaries** (church Scripture readings). The job of comparing manuscripts can be rather tedious and time consuming, and in fact, has never been completely done. Instead, theories and principles have been devised to apply to the texts that we possess in an effort to hasten the process, or to shortcut some of the required steps.

B.   Why Textual Criticism Is Needed

When the Apostles wrote down God's inspired Word, the very product itself, even the spelling of each word, was God-breathed (2 Tim 3:16). There were no mistakes of grammar, or errors of fact whatsoever. God did not guarantee, however, a perfect transmission of those original texts. Instead, no two copies are completely alike. In the various copies small variations frequently occur in spelling, word order, syntax, and in numerous other ways. Preservation of the perfect original has not occurred, nor is it taught in the Bible, or expected to be the case. That is why textual criticism is needed--to help determine the original text.

For example, if thirty second graders each copied the teacher's letter to the President, and then the original was lost--how could it ever be recovered? The thirty copies could be compared. That exercise would uncover misspelled words, some omitted words, and other usual types of mistakes. However, the original wording probably could be determined, even if *each copy* had several errors. The textual criticism of the New Testament is somewhat like that, only much larger in both scope and depth. The types of changes introduced into copies fall into two primary categories.

1.   *Unintentional Changes.* Some copyist mistakes were completely unintentional and occurred for a number of quite normal reasons. It is always possible to mistake one Greek letter for another. The only difference between a sigma (C), and an epsilon (E) was a tiny line. So with the theta (Θ) and the omicron (O). The

gamma ($\mathcal{T}$), pi ($\mathcal{\Pi}$), and tau ($\mathcal{T}$) all looked similar enough to cause occasional confusion for a tired scribe, and so did the lambda ($\wedge$) and the delta ($\triangle$), or two lambdas ($\wedge\wedge$) and a mu ($\mathcal{M}$), or a lambda-iota combination ($\wedge I$) with a nu (N).

Frequently, Greek words end with the same letters much like the English *--ing, --ment, --ed, --tion,* or *--ity.* When that occurs it is easy for a scribe to jump on to the next word or line that ends with the same letters. Once in a while a copyist writes a word twice when it should occur only once. Some errors were made from hearing one word but writing another that sounds the same but is spelled differently-- like *deer, dear*; or *pair, pare, pear*; or *road, rode.* On occasion a scribe would accidentally invert letters or whole words, substitute synonyms, or write a passage more from memory than from copying!

2. *Intentional Changes.* Intentional changes in the text were also made in the copying process. Sometimes a scribe would change the spelling or syntax to conform to that with which he was familiar. Changes were sometimes made to eliminate apparent discrepancies, or to harmonize one Gospel with another. If copying from and comparing two different manuscripts how was the scribe to distinguish between their possible differences? Sometimes he simply may have copied both into the text (*conflation*). A zealous scribe may have sought to correct what he considered to be an error in a manuscript, but instead created one of his own. There were also doctrinal changes purposely introduced to advance some heresy or false teaching. Finally, some manuscripts have extra details added in-- such as the supposed name of the rich man (Luke

16:19), or the name of Cleopas' walking companion on the road to Emmaus (Luke 24:18).

II.   THE MATERIALS OF TEXTUAL CRITICISM

Parts of the New Testament have been found written on a few ostraca (pieces of broken pottery) and some talismans, but most are contained on *papyri*, *vellum*, or *parchment* (calf or deer skins), and some later ones on paper. The earliest are the papyri, (2nd-8th centuries), and the uncials (4th-9th centuries), followed by the cursives (9th-16th centuries), and the lectionaries (6th century on). The versions or translations into other languages also bear some testimony as to the Greek text, as does the use the church fathers made of the New Testament in their writings.

A.   Papyri Manuscripts

The first non-biblical papyrus manuscript was found in Egypt before 1800, but until 1865 none of the New Testament was contained on any of the new discoveries. Today more than 115 papyri manuscripts (some just fragments) have been uncovered that contain over 40 percent of the New Testament including part of every book except 2 Tim. Most date prior to the fifth century. Papyrus manuscripts are listed and referred to by a large P with a superscript number attached. The most famous are P^{45} P^{46} P^{52} P^{66} P^{72} P^{74} P^{75}. The earliest, P^{52}, is called the John Rylands fragment, and contains only a few verses from a page of John's Gospel (18:31-33, 37-38), but it is dated about A.D. 125.

P45-P47 form the Chester Beatty collection. P45 has 13 pages of Acts 5:30-17:17, while P46 has about 90 leaves containing most of Rom, Heb, 1 and 2 Cor, Gal, Eph, Phil, Col, and 1 Thess. The ten leaves of P47 have about one-third of Rev (9:10-17:2). The pages are about 9½ by 5½ inches, written on both sides with 25-30 lines per page. The Beatty manuscripts are dated fairly early (3rd century).

P66, P72, and P74-75 are known as the Bodmer collection. Two-thirds of John's Gospel is contained on about 75 leaves (printed on both sides) of P66, dated about A.D. 200 or possibly earlier. P72 has 1 and 2 Peter and Jude (3rd century), while P74 has fragments of Acts and some of the catholic or general epistles (6th or 7th century). P75 was a much used copy of about half of Luke and John dating from A.D. 200. These are extremely early witnesses to the text.

B. Uncial Manuscripts

About 325 uncial manuscripts have been uncovered. These are designated by *names* (Sinaiticus, Vaticanus), *capital letters* of the English and Greek alphabet (A, B, C, Δ, Θ, π, ϕ, plus the Hebrew letter $\aleph$), and by *Arabic numerals preceded by a zero* (01, 02, 08, 0250). The word uncial (inch high) refers to the practice of printing large capital letters without spaces between the words. John 10:30 would read "IANDMYFATHERAREONE," while John 3:30 would read "HEMUSTINCREASEBUTIMUST DECREASE." Manuscript space was expensive in those days, but the Greek reader could read such printing fairly well.

Some of the earlier and more famous uncial manuscripts are noted below. **Aleph** (01, $\aleph$,

Sinaiticus) was obtained by Constantine Tischendorf in 1859 from the Monastery of St. Catherine on Mt. Sinai. Its 147½ New Testament pages measure 15 x 13½ inches with four narrow columns on each page running 48 lines per column. It also has 199 leaves of the Old Testament. The date of Sinaiticus is about A.D. 340. The text is clearly printed and easy to read. The British Museum now owns 01.

Alexandrinus (02, A), dates from the 5th century and has 143 New Testament leaves measuring 10 x 13 inches (besides 630 Old Testament pages). Only two long columns of 46-52 lines a piece are on each page. The manuscript was given to Charles I of England in 1627 and it rests next to א$ in the British Museum.

Vaticanus (03, B) is dated early 4th century and rests in the Vatican Library. It contains most of the New Testament, but lacks the pastorals, Philem, Rev, and Heb 9:14-13:25. Its pages are 11 x 11 inches with three columns of 40-44 lines each per page.

Ephraemi Rescriptus (04, C) is a *palimpsest*. The Greek Bible text was scraped off the parchment and the sermons of Ephraemi were written over that text. It contains parts of almost every New Testament book on its 145 leaves (N.T.) with only one column per page (each line has about 40 characters). C is in the National Library of Paris and is dated in the 5th century.

Bezae (05, D) is a bilingual manuscript (Greek on left, Latin on right) and has most of the Gospels--Matt, John, Luke, and Mark (in that order, Apostles first)--and Acts. It received its name when Theodore Beza presented the manuscript to Cambridge University in 1581.

Other important uncial codex (book form) manuscripts are Washingtonianus (032, W), a 4th

The Six Types of Manuscript Evidence

1. PAPYRI

Manuscripts written on papyrus usually appear in capital letters. 118 or more of these mss, all designated by a large letter "P" with a superscript number.

$$P^{45} \quad P^{72} \quad P^{52} \quad P^{74} \quad P^{47} \quad P^{1} \quad P^{75} \quad P^{118}$$

2. UNCIALS

Manuscripts written in large, capital letters, usually on parchment or vellum, between the IV-VIII centuries. They are designated by capital letters of English and Greek and by a cardinal number preceded by zero. About 325 are known.

$$A, \ B, \ C, \ D, \ \Delta, \ \Pi, \ \Psi, \ 05, \ 0142, \ 0256, \ 015, \ Z, \ H.$$

3. MINISCULES OR CURSIVES

Manuscripts written in a cursive handwriting between the IX-XVI centuries. About 3,000 are known. They are designated by cardinal numbers.

$$1, \ 69, \ 113, \ 209, \ 2456, \ 33, \ 565, \ 1010, \ 700, \ \textit{etc.}$$

If the bulk of all cursives is meant, the symbol **Byz.** is used

4. LECTIONARIES

About 2,500 mss. are known that served as Church readings of Scripture, such as the ones in the back of many modern hymnals. They date from the VI century on, and are designated by a small, cursive ℓ with a superscript number. If the bulk of all lectionaries are meant, the symbol **Lect.** is used.

$$\ell^{25} \quad \ell^{250} \quad \ell^{782} \quad \ell^{1116} \quad \ell^{1900} \quad \text{Lect.} \quad \ell^{1} \quad \ell^{5}$$

5. VERSIONS

The ancient versions or translations of New Testament Greek text appeared as early as the II century. They are abbreviated.

it = old Latin   cop = Coptic   goth = Gothic   eth = Ethiopic
syr = Syriac   vg = Vulgate   geo = Georgian   arm = Armenian

6. CHURCH FATHERS

The names of the church fathers are written out in full. It is important to know where they lived and when they lived as they give witness to the text.

or 5th century copy of the Gospels; Koridethianus (038, Θ) of the Gospels; Claromontanus (06, D2) the Pauline epistles (6th century); Cyprius (017, K), 267 leaves of the Gospels (9th or 10th century); Regius (019, L), an 8th century Gospels manuscript with two columns on each of its 257 8½ x 6½ inch pages. There are more than 250 other uncials as well.

C.   Minuscule or Cursive Manuscripts

There are nearly 3,000 extant minuscule manuscripts. They are numbered simply from 1 on up--26, 61, 189, 565, 1012, 2495, etc. These date from the 9th to the 16th centuries and were copies of earlier uncial manuscripts, and later on perhaps of other minuscules. The writing is in a flowing cursive Greek script, the purposes of which were to save (1) space, and (2) time in copying. Too bad Xerox did not make its appearance earlier. Father Dominick could have really saved time and made fewer mistakes as well.

The cursive codexes no doubt represent every part of the world and demonstrate how basically uniform the text was that they copied. Several of these 3,000 copies are from two separate sub-families that are called Family 1 and Family 13. Family 1 contains 1, 118, 131, 209, and 1582. Family 13 contains 13, 69, 124, 346, 543, 788, 826, 828 and some others. f13 is distinct because the woman taken in adultery passage is placed between Luke 21 and 22. That section generally comes in John 7:53-8:11. The rest of the thousands of cursives are all distinct and each one brings a separate witness to the New Testament text. The King James, and the New King James Versions were translated primarily from manuscripts representing this large body of cursives. Most of the newer translations (from 1881 on) have been based on fewer but earlier manuscripts, and so they differ. This will be explained further in chapter 15.

D. Lectionary Manuscripts

There are in existence today more than 2,430 lectionary manuscripts available today. They date as early as the 6th century (fragments), but the earliest complete copy is from the 8th century. Many were written in uncial characters, but most are in cursive style. About 600 are from the epistles, 75 combine Gospels and epistles, and the remaining 1,500 or so are of the Gospels alone. Work on the lectionaries has not been extensive in the past, but their immense value for textual criticism has been increasingly recognized. These manuscripts were what the churches used for Scripture reading before Bibles were "in print." Thus, these manuscripts were the only Bible many knew for a thousand years.

E. Versions

The Greek New Testament was translated into many different languages and these versions bear some testimony to the original text. They can be dated fairly well, and they do portray the text used in a certain area of the church. Naturally, since they are in languages different from Greek, they cannot always tell us what Greek words were translated, but they can witness to additions, omissions, and the general direction of the text. The Syriac, Latin, and Coptic were several of the primary versions. Some of these are quite extensive, the Latin Vulgate being contained in no less than 8,000 manuscripts.

The **Syriac versions** date back to the 2nd century with the Sinaitic and Curetonian Syriac texts. Three others, the Peshitta (common), Philoxenian and Harklean, and Palestinian Syriac may be dated somewhat later, perhaps as late as the 5th century for some although some opinions might place the Peshitta Syriac version considerably earlier. The Peshitta was the standard text and is found in about 350 manuscripts, whereas most of the others are in fragments or very few manuscripts. The notations for the Syriac versions are Syr[s,c,p,ph,har,pal]. The superscript letters stand for the *different translations* of the Syriac just mentioned.

There are two **Latin versions**--the Old Latin dating from around A.D. 150-200, and the Latin Vulgate (common), translated by Jerome around A.D. 400. Several manuscripts of the Old Latin, it[a] (Vercellensis) and it[k] (Bobiensis), are about as early as Aleph and B, the two oldest uncial manuscripts. The Latin Vulgate comes in two editions, the Wordsworth and White (Vg[ww]), and the Clementine (Vg[Clem]). It was and is *the* Bible for the Western church (Roman Catholic).

In Egypt, the **Coptic** language was used to make several translations of the New Testament. The Sahidic and Bohairic dialects date from about A.D. 200, although the earliest manuscripts known today are from the 6th and 7th centuries. Other Coptic dialects were the Fayyumic and Achmimic. There are noted as Cop[sa,bo,fay,ach].

Other later versions include **Gothic** (4th century), **Armenian** (5th century), **Georgian** (5th century), **Ethiopic** (4th to 7th centuries), **Arabic**, **Nubian**, and others.

F.   Quotations from the Fathers

The church fathers also bear an important testimony to the text that they used, although it is not complete, but scattered in various comments they made on different passages. However, these men can be dated fairly accurately and represent particular localities. In general, they are very early--some earlier than the oldest papyri, and many coming before the earliest uncials. Therefore, they can play a key role in helping to establish the original text. Naturally, sometimes they may have paraphrased or quoted from memory. On occasion, they cite a verse two different ways. All these factors must be considered.

These then are the materials for textual criticism--the comparing of manuscripts to determine what the true text was. Their *use* is discussed in the following chapter (13) on theory, and some application of theory is practiced in chapter 14.

III.   FOR REVIEW AND DISCUSSION

1. Give a concise definition of what textual criticism is. What is its purpose and how is it accomplished?

2. Discuss whether and/or why textual criticism is needed. Do we have the original manuscripts today? Are any of our copies without error? Did God ever promise to supernaturally preserve the text (and if so how?), or does He expect us to use textual criticism to preserve and maintain the text?

3. List and distinguish between the various kinds of unintentional and intentional changes that scribes may have introduced into the text.

4. List and describe the materials available for textual criticism under the six major types of evidence, *i.e.*, papyri, uncials, minuscules, lectionaries, etc.

IV. FOR FURTHER READING AND RESEARCH

Aland, Barbara and Kurt. *The Text of the New Testament: An Introduction to the Critical Editions and to the Theory and Practices of Modern Textual Criticism.* 2nd ed. Grand Rapids: Eerdmans, 1989.

Aland, Barbara, Kurt Aland, Johannes Karavidopoulos, Carlo M. Martini, and Bruce M. Metzger, Eds. *The Greek New Testament.* Stuttgart: Deutsche Bibelgesellschaft, 2005.

Burgon, John William. *The Causes of the Corruption of the Traditional Text of the Holy Gospels.* Ed. Edward Miller. London: George Bell, 1896. xvi + 290.

Comfort, Philip W. and David Barrett. *The Complete Text of the Earliest New Testament Manuscripts.* Grand Rapids: Baker, 1999.

Ehrman, Bart D. and Michael W. Holmes. *The Text of the New Testament in Contemporary Research: Essays on the Status Quaestionis.* Grand Rapids: Eerdmans, 1995. xiv + 401.

Finegan, Jack. *Encountering New Testament Manuscripts.* Grand Rapids: Eerdmans, 1974. 203 pp.

Head, Peter M. "P. Bodmer II (P[66]): Three Fragments Identified." *Novum Testamentum* 47 (2005) 2:105-108.

Mitchell, Margaret M. and Patricia A. Duncan. "Chicago's 'Archaic Mark' (MS 2427): A Reintroduction to Its Enigmas and a Fresh Collation of Its Readings." *Novum Testamentum* 48 (2006) 1:1-35

Nicklas, Tobias. "Papyrus Egerton 2—the 'Unknown Gospel.'" *Expository Times* 118 (2007) 6:261-266.

13

THEORIES OF
TEXTUAL CRITICISM

I. THE RISE OF THE
CRITICAL TEXT

A. The First Printed Editions

The first edited and printed Greek text was produced by the great Renaissance scholar Erasmus in 1516. He compared more than a dozen of the best manuscripts he could find in an effort to engage in textual criticism rather than merely recopying a single manuscript with its errors. His text went through little change in five editions. Later in the same century, Robert Estienne, a French printer, commonly called Stephanus, published four editions of the Greek New Testament based primarily on Erasmus' fifth edition. Theodore Beza edited ten editions of the Greek New Testament between 1565-1611. In 1633, the Elzevir brothers (Bonaventure and Abraham), published an edition with a printer's blurb in Latin that claimed it was *the text received* everywhere in the world. Their edition was commonly referred to as the Textus Receptus (Received Text, or TR). It was the standard for the next two and a half centuries (1630-1880).

B.   Further Research and Discovery

Both the Renaissance and the Reformation opened scholars up to the past and renewed study and research were directed into Hebrew and Greek. More manuscripts became known, and eventually it was discovered that a few early manuscripts contained a text that differed in many small ways from the text based on the relatively later manuscripts used by Erasmus, Stephanus, Beza, and the Elzevir brothers. The researches of John Fell (1625-1686), John Mill (1645-1707), Richard Bentley (1662-1742), Johann Bengal (1687-1752), and others gave indications of this "earlier" text, but their efforts were isolated and did not affect the tide of scholarship in their day.

However, between 1830-1880, more manuscripts were collated (differences noted), and the work of Griesbach (1745-1812), Lachmann (1794-1852), Tregelles (1813-1875), and Tischendorf (1815-1874) resulted in a more scholarly awareness of the basic differences between manuscripts and even groups of manuscripts. It remained for two British scholars, however, to put forth a textual theory that would dethrone the Textus Receptus, and replace it with a text based on supposedly older and better manuscripts.

C.   The Work of Westcott and Hort

B. F. Westcott (1825-1901), and F. J. A. Hort (1828-1892), worked for twenty-five years on manuscripts and a textual theory to explain manuscript differences. They concluded that all New Testament Greek manuscripts fell into one of four basic text types: (1) **Western,** used in Rome and the Western church, particularly reflected in

Codex D and the Latin; (2) **Syrian,** originating in Antioch of Syria and used primarily by the Eastern churches of Constantinople, Asia Minor and Greece; (3) **Alexandrian,** from Alexandria, Egypt; and a (4) **Neutral** text, reflected in several relatively "pure" manuscripts.

Westcott and Hort published their Greek text in 1881-82 in time for it to be used in the revision of the King James Version (1881-1885). The result was the English Revised Version of 1881, (and the American Standard Version, 1901), excellent, very literal translations, but based on a text of the New Testament that differed from the TR in several thousand instances.

The principles that led Westcott and Hort to their adoption of a *minority* text were explained in the introduction to their Greek text. They held that (1) the Syrian type text resulted from a 4th century revision of earlier texts--namely the Western and Alexandrian. This was supposedly proven by conflation (adding two earlier texts together to form one longer expanded version), and by the idea that no early church father or manuscript ever gave witness to an exclusively Syrian reading or variant. Both the conflation question and the quotation by church fathers issues are hotly debated. Both logic and later papyri discoveries demonstrate the weakness of this point, and no trace of a supposed revision can be found in any records of church history. Many feel the "revision" concept was a *fiction* used to cast off the Textus Receptus. Westcott and Hort held that the Syrian text, as they termed the *85-90% majority of all Greek texts,* could be eliminated from consideration since it was obviously a derivation from other earlier texts. (2) When either the Western or Alexandrian texts agree with the Neutral text, that reading was preferred. (3) If the

Western, Alexandrian, and Neutral differed--the Neutral was still to be preferred (almost always). The manuscript containing the Neutral text was B, or Vaticanus. In practical terms, the text of Westcott and Hort was the text of B.

Much of Westcott and Hort's theory was based on *circular reasoning*. They reasoned that (1) the best readings are found in the best manuscripts, and (2) the best manuscripts are the ones that have the best readings. Which readings (or variants when two texts differ) are *best* is an *assumption* used to prove which manuscripts are best. Likewise, which manuscripts are best is an assumption used to prove which readings are best. It is similar to the evolutionist's argument that (1) evolution is proven by the great age of the fossils and conversely (2) the great age of the fossils is proven by evolution. Both are unwarranted assumptions.

II.   PRINCIPLES OF TEXTUAL EVIDENCE

A.   Principles of Transcriptional Evidence

A number of principles are generally accepted as providing an objective basis for choosing between differing readings in manuscripts. These principles seek to explain how the errors may have arisen in the process of transcribing or copying a manuscript.

1. *The reading which best explains the rise of all others in a given passage is preferred*. This may require some careful thinking. Could an obscure word give rise to several easier terms? Could a particular Greek letter or word have been

misread in copying, resulting in an unusual or difficult expression? Did a scribe doze off and forget to complete a word or phrase? Did a copyist skip a line or a word? Was an explanation added to the text? All these questions and many others may yield fruitful results.

2. *Generally, the shorter reading is preferred.* This principle is based on the idea that scribes tended to add to rather than to omit material. Just the opposite, however, may have been the case. Over the years, those who have transcribed my papers, letters, or theses, have rarely added, but frequently have omitted words, even whole lines, and occasionally paragraphs. The eye and hand more easily skip (accidentally) than they add. The critical text found in the few manuscripts is a *shorter* text. Many hundreds of words and even whole phrases are missing. Either the majority text (W & H's Syrian text) *added* a significant amount, or else there were a few manuscripts that survived which contained a text with not a few deletions and omissions.

3. *Generally, the more difficult reading is preferred.* The reason for this dictum is the thought that scribes tend to simplify what lies before them. However, what is considered difficult or simple might be a matter of opinion. With several different writers producing the New Testament, what was difficult for one may have been simple for the next. Who is to say? Then again, any common error may turn a simple phrase into a rather difficult rendering. The caution here is that a difficult reading which makes no sense is beyond the limits of this principle.

B.   The Principle of Intrinsic Probability

Transcriptional probability considers what a **scribe** might have done with the text at hand, but *intrinsic probability* considers what the **author** might have been more likely to write. As such, the latter can lack objectivity. This principle claims that *the reading is preferred which best fits the author's characteristic tendencies.* But how can one be certain about what a writer *would* have said in a particular place? Hopefully, any application of intrinsic probability would match the findings of transcriptional probability--but who can tell? Care must be exercised in both realms.

III.   THE PRINCIPLES OF TOTAL CONSIDERATION

Most scholars at the time of Westcott and Hort accepted and repeated their theory. Some doubted and questioned, while others flatly rejected it. One of those who engaged in the debate opposing the views of Westcott and Hort was John W. Burgon, Dean of Chichester. He felt, along with Scrivener, Salmon, Miller, Cook and others that the new *theory* all too conveniently discarded the great majority of **manuscript** evidence (the only *real* evidence for the text there is) in favor of the text to be found in a few early copies. In order to secure a more reasoned consideration of the total wealth of evidence, Dean Burgon proposed what he called seven "Tests of Truth."[1] These are condensed below.

---

[1] These appear on pp. 40-67 of Burgon's *The Traditional Text of the Holy Gospels*, and are repeated in *True or False?* ed. by David O. Fuller, and in Wilbur N. Pickering's *The Identity of the New Testament Text*. See section VI for each of these.

A.   Antiquity

Although the oldest manuscript may not contain the oldest text, there is a probability that the older manuscripts may better approximate the original than do later copies that may be the results of material copied twenty times over. But it should be remembered that most errors appeared in the copies during the first century of the copying process--so an old copy is not necessarily a good copy. In addition, a 12th century manuscript may be a good copy of an 8th century copy of a good 3rd century text; while a 5th century manuscript could be as many as ten or twenty copies removed from the original.

But, in general, antiquity, though not the sole criterion, must be considered a vital point in evaluating the manuscript evidence. Antiquity would be material of the 4th century or earlier and would include such items as Codexes Aleph and Vaticanus, some of the papyri, a number of the versions, and a whole host of church fathers.

B.   Number

In order to overthrow the testimony of the many witnesses that speak with a concerted voice, many critics have recommended that manuscripts are to be weighed, not counted. The critic of large numbers of manuscripts would suggest that a few good manuscripts should be given more weight than the many others. But this overlooks the reality that a large factor in weight is number itself.

If there are fewer than 450 papyri and uncials combined, out of over 5,750 separate Greek manuscripts, is this point automatically to go to the reading contained in the later more numerous copies? Before one answers that question, he must ask himself where the more numerous 8th and 9th or 10th and 11th century copies came from. They were themselves, in many cases no doubt, copies of other earlier papyri and uncials. Each miniscule bears a separate and individual testimony, with the exception of Family 1 and Family 13 where several copies are closely related. A single uncial may be worth more than four or five cursives, but is it to be valued more than scores or even hundreds of other witnesses? Number must be considered as an important factor, but only as *one* of the tests of truth.

C. Variety

The greater the variety of witnesses there are, the less chance there is for collusion or deceit to spring from the few. Variety may be exhibited by differences in locality as well as age. Only rarely can it be told with accuracy from where a particular manuscript may have come. Witnesses from east, west, north, and south are invited to bear separate testimony. In this regard the various versions and church fathers are valuable in showing variety, but so must be the variety attesting the reading supported by greater numbers as well.

D. Weight or Respectability

Burgon also would have us consider the weight of each particular witness, a point for which many scholars contend. But respectability is different from being an oracle. If a manuscript proves itself to be erroneous on a frequent basis by a number of acceptable standards, then it loses its respectability. If a manuscript is proven to be a mere copy of another as Tischendorf suspected E was of Clarmontanus, or as 102 was of B, then its weight as an *independent* witness is voided. In addition, fathers who merely quote each other have no weight of their own, anymore than do the individual manuscripts of Families 1 or 13. Burgon would add that a church father bears a testimony of a particular date and region, while an ancient uncial's testimony carries certainty about neither.

E. Continuity

Another factor to consider in the manuscript evidence is that of the continuity of witnesses. Does a particular reading have at least some unbroken testimony down through the ages or is it a reading that was abandoned long ago. A chasm or a hiatus in the chain of evidence is not a good sign. One need not have overwhelming numbers on his side to merit this point, but there must be some showing of continuous evidence through the centuries.

F. Context

Another criterion by which to evaluate individual manuscripts is that of context. This means to see whether a particular manuscript bears credible testimony in and around the passage in question. Codex D, for example, varies from anyone's standard to a certain average degree in Luke 1-21. But in chapters 22-24, the text of D varies considerably from any standard text one might care to use. His testimony is thereby rendered suspect by the *context* of the surrounding chapters. This point requires careful in-depth study and might only be applied by hours of study spent on each manuscript, but it is nonetheless a salient point--though not as readily applicable as the other tests of truth.

G. Reasonableness

A final note of truth is the consideration of reasonableness. If a particular reading is grammatically, geographically, scientifically, or historically impossible, then it must not be accepted, if other readings do not present such problems. For example, codices Aleph, I, K, N, and 𝜋 give the distance in Luke 24:13 from Jerusalem to Emmaus as 160 furlongs (a geographical impossibility) instead of 60 which is correct. Those readings and others like them must be ruled out by the internal evidence of reasonableness.

In conclusion, all seven tests of truth may not agree in substantiating one reading over another, but if one variant has a very sizeable majority of these factors on its side, the weight of probability is thrown its way.

IV. A NOTE ON CONFLATIONS

A *conflation* is supposed to be the copying together of two different sources to make one new (and expanded) reading. Westcott and Hort gave eight examples (yet claimed many more) in an attempt to substantiate their theory that the majority manuscripts (Syrian or Byzantine text types) were much *later manuscripts* and therefore of no consequence to textual criticism. This would be a devasting charge if it could be proven--but it cannot be proven with any certainty.

Luke 24:53 is the classic example given by Westcott and Hort to prove conflation in the majority texts. A few manuscripts, P⁷⁵, ℵ ,B, C, L and several versions, have the Christians in the temple "blessing" God after the ascension. D, some Old Latin copies, and Augustine have them "praising" God instead. But, the great majority of all manuscripts, uncials, cursives, lectionaries, and versions have *both* "praising and blessing." Does the combination of words prove derivation and lateness? On the contrary, it may more easily be seen to prove just the opposite.

If "blessing" was the original word, then where and how did "praising" come to replace it completely in a few manuscripts? Contrariwise, if "praising" was the God-breathed word, then who replaced it with "blessing?" It is just as easy to suggest and believe that the huge majority of all manuscripts and versions are correct when they indicate "praising and blessing." The two *single* readings could easily have arisen by a careless scribe omitting one or other of the words, since they both end with the same six Greek letters (*ountes*).

V. FOR REVIEW AND DISCUSSION

1. Who were the primary movers behind some of the first printed editions of the Greek New Testament, and about when did they do their work?
2. Name some of the men who largely favored the text found in the earlier manuscripts but were unsuccessful in moving scholarship totally in that direction.
3. Discuss the textual theory of Westcott and Hort. What were their four text types? How did

conflation fit into their theory? Did they favor a majority or a minority text? Why?

4. List, explain, and discuss the pro's and con's of the various principles of transcriptional and intrinsic probability.

5. List, explain, and discuss the seven principles of total consideration or tests of truth. Do they make sense? Do you believe it is proper to apply such tests to places where manuscripts differ on possible readings? Why or why not?

VI.   FOR FURTHER READING AND RESEARCH

Burgon, John William. *The Traditional Text of the Holy Gospels Vindicated and Established*. Ed. Edward Miller. London: George Bell, 1896. xx + 317.

Comfort, Philip Wesley. *The Quest for the Original Text of the New Testament*. Grand Rapids: Baker, 1992. 200 pp.

Ellis, E. Earle. *The Making of the New Testament Documents*. Leiden: Brill, 1999. xxiv + 522.

Epp, Eldon Jay and Gordon D. Fee. *Studies in the Theory and Method of New Testament Textual Criticism*. Grand Rapids: Eerdmans, 1993. xiv + 414.

Fee, Gordon D. "Modern Textual Criticism and the Revival of the Textus Receptus." *Journal of the Evangelical Theological Society*. 21:1 (March, 1978): 19-34.

Fuller, David Otis, ed. *True or False? The Westcott-Hort Textual Theory Explained*. Grand Rapids: Grand Rapids International, 1973. 295 pp.

Greenlee, J. Harold. *Introduction to New Testament Textual Criticism*. Rev. ed. Peabody, MA: Hendrickson Publishers, 1995. xii + 160.

Hodges, Zane C. "Modern Textual Criticism and the Majority Text: A Response." *Journal of the Evangelical Theological Society*. 21:2 (June, 1978): 143-156.

Kenyon, Frederic George. *Our Bible and the Ancient Manuscripts.* 3rd ed. London: Eyre and Spottiswoode, 1897. xii + 255.

_____. *The Text of the Greek Bible.* 2nd ed. London: Duckworth, 1948. 264 pp.

Metzger, Bruce Manning. *The Text of the New Testament Its Transmission, Corruption, and Restoration.* 3rd enl. Ed. New York: Oxford University Press, 1992. ix + 310.

Miller, Edward. *A Guide to the Textual Criticism of the New Testament.* London: George Bell, 1886. xiv + 147.

Parvis, Merrill M. "Text, New Testament." *The Interpreter's Dictionary of the Bible.* Ed. G. A. Buttrick. Nashville: Abingdon, 1962. IV, 594-614.

Pickering, Wilbur N. *The Identity of the New Testament Text.* Nashville: Thomas Nelson, 1977. 249 pp.

Salmon, George. *Some Thoughts on the Textual Criticism of the New Testament.* London: John Murray, 1897.

Scrivener, F. H. A. *A Plain Introduction to the Criticism of the New Testament.* London: George Bell, 1894. 2 vols.

Sturz, Harry A. *The Byzantine Text-Type and New Testament Textual Criticism.* Nashville: Thomas Nelson, 1984. 305 pp.

Wegner, Paul D. *A Student's Guide to Textual Criticism of the Bible.* Downers Grove, IL: InterVarsity Press, 2006. 334 pp.

Westcott, Brooke Foss and Fenton John Anthony Hort. *The New Testament in the Original Greek.* New York: Harper, 1882.

14

HOW TO SOLVE TEXTUAL PROBLEMS

I. THE METHOD TO USE

Solving textual problems is a complex rather than a simple task. One must have a certain knowledge of the evidence before he can begin to evaluate it. This involves a detailed study of manuscripts, the symbols that represent them, types of scribal changes, theories of textual transmission, principles for evaluating competing readings (variants), and a method for applying those principles. The textual theory to which one subscribes may provide certain presuppositions that will circumscribe one's treatment of the evidence.

For example, Westcott and Hort gave little place to readings supported by the majority manuscripts when they opposed a reading of Aleph and B, because of their high regard for those two "neutral" manuscripts (a question-begging title). They were so certain of their position that they titled their book *The New Testament in **the** Original Greek*. Imagine, rediscovering the text of the very autographs!

Burgon, on the other hand, had a poor opinion of Aleph and B. He was convinced that since the true text was the *only* text copied at the beginning, that fact accounted for its multiplication into the majority, while the few copies of the "neutral"text indicated that it was a later offshoot. Although Burgon did not believe the TR was without its faults, he felt it was superior to the critical minority text of Westcott and Hort. The grandchild of Westcott and Hort's critical text has been used in translating every recognized modern version since 1881--*ASV, RSV, NASB, NEB, TEV,* and *NIV*--with the sole exception of the NKJV which is based on the Textus Receptus as a revision of the KJV.

There are some, however, who believe that the Textus Receptus of 1633 (essentially that on which the KJV was based earlier) has the quality of being God-breathed. This belief is maintained apart from scriptural warrant, but frees its devotees from all efforts of textual criticism. Ignoring all manuscript differences, this view places a mystic faith in the Greek text arranged by such fallible men as Erasmus, Stephanus, Beza, and the Elzevir brothers.

The method employed in this chapter is that of applying to each variant reading, at least in a cursory fashion, the seven *tests of truth* listed on previous pages. This will give a good idea as to what the evidence is and what it means. Three problems have been selected: one from the Gospels; one from Acts; and one from the epistles. The first demonstrates an example of poor character in Aleph and B; the second shows a major flaw in the Textus Receptus; and the third illustrates how minor some of the differences can be.

II. THREE SELECTED TEXTUAL PROBLEMS

A. Matthew 27:49

Just before Jesus cried out with a loud voice and yielded up His spirit (Matt 27:50), the crowd said, "Let Him alone, let us see if Elijah will come to save Him" (Matt 27:49). Almost all manuscripts--early, late, and otherwise--show the text to be as it stands above. This includes uncials A, D, K, W, Δ , Θ , π ,and 090, plus the cursives of family 1 and 13, 28, 33, 565, 700, 892, 1009, 1071, 1079, etc.--the giant bulk of the Byzantine Majority; the bulk of all lectionaries, the Old Latin, the Vulgate, the Peshitta, Sinaitic, Harklean, and manuscripts of the Palestinian Syriac, plus the Gothic, Armenian, and Georgian versions, and the Diatessaron (A.D. 170). Church fathers on this side of the question are Origen, Eusebius, Hilary, Jerome, Augustine and the Apostolic Canons.

Opposite this evidence are a few sources which have some **additional words** *between* verses 49 and 50. They say, "But another taking a lance pricked his side and there came out water and blood." These additional words are a poor rendition of John 19:34. They are contained here *only* in Aleph, B, C, L, 1010, some manuscripts of the Palestinian Syriac, a manuscript of the Ethiopic, and in Chrysostom (according to Severus).

Let us now apply the seven tests of truth. (1) *Antiquity* is clearly one-sided, being witnessed for the majority reading by all early versions and the church fathers, as well as numerous 5th century uncials. (2) *Number* is also obviously in favor of the first reading. (3) *Variety* supports the initial reading, as does (4) *respectability*. The witnesses for the additional words lose some of their respectability based on this one reading alone, as will be seen in point #7. (5) *Continuity* is completely lost in the second reading, while perfectly maintained in the first. It is not hard to see why intelligent copyists avoided the second worthless reading. (6) The *context* surrounding this verse in each manuscript cannot be researched easily, so this point is mute--although it would be good know in some cases. (7) The second reading is ***totally impossible*** based on its *reasonableness*. Jesus was supposed to have been **dead** when the soldiers pierced His side with a lance. But here one of the crowd, not a soldier, takes a lance and pierces it into Jesus' side. Out comes blood and water (instead of water and blood as John 19:34 has it)--signs of death--yet this **minority text** says in verse 50 that Jesus cried out *after that,* and then yielded up His spirit. This would clearly be a logical, medical, and scriptural absurdity.

A very embarrassing fact must be faced by Westcott and Hort (who left the passage bracketed *in* their text) and others who admire Aleph and B. *Only* five Greek manuscripts contain the addition--four uncials and a lone cursive. Their scribes apparently followed a defective text at this point and were witless enough to copy it right into their own manuscripts. And is it not strange that no one after these few (that we know of) copied from them or from the defective copy they used (at least on this verse)?

B. Acts 9:5-6

Every Greek manuscript in existence which contains the Book of Acts (except one, minuscule

629), does not have the several additional sentences that are found in some of the Old Latin, the Clementine Vulgate, and four of the church fathers in Acts 9:5-6.

Acts 9 tells of Saul's conversion on the Damascus road, which is repeated as a personal testimony in Acts 22 and 26. One of the additional sentences in question is contained in Acts 26:14, "it is hard for you to kick against the goads." Only one manuscript, a bilingual Greek-Latin text, cursive 629, contains those words in *Greek*. Some additional words of Acts 9:6 apparently are recomposed from Acts 22:10, "So I said, 'What shall I do Lord?' and the Lord said to me." An additional phrase, "So he, trembling and astonished" is only found in Latin. **No** Greek manuscript of Acts 9:6 contains either these words, or the words of Acts 22:10.

To narrow the discussion somewhat, let us consider the seven tests of truth. (1) *Antiquity* does not favor the additional words. P⁷⁵, ℵ (Aleph), A, B, C, E, P, Ψ, 049, 056, and 0142 lack the words, as do the Wordsworth and White edition of the Vulgate, the Coptic, Armenian, and Chrysostom. The only early support for the added words are several Old Latin copies, the Clementine Vulgate, Lucifer, Ephraem, and Ambrose (all fathers from the late 4th century). (2) Regarding *number,* only one Greek manuscript contains a few of the words of 9:5, while **all** others do not. (3) *Variety* is found truly only in the more than 99 percent of manuscripts which omit the dubious clauses. (4) Bilingual Codex 629's *respectability* is greatly suspect where its Greek text seems to follow the spurious addition of its corresponding Latin page. (5) *Continuity* is almost totally lacking in support of the additional words. Codex 629 is perhaps a 14th century copy. Where is the intervening Greek support (before or after)? There is none. (6) The *context* of 629 is suspicious, because its Latin text contains the questioned reading and so the Greek traces its error for a few words. (7) There is nothing *unreasonable* about the additional words or their omission. Either would be appropriate, but it is easy to see how a harmonistic transfer may have occurred between Acts 22:10, 26:14 and Latin copies of 9:5-6.

The embarrassing point about this text is that the Textus Receptus *contains* it! All Greek manuscript evidence omits it, but the TR includes fifteen extra words! The Greek part of Codex 629 only supports five of the Greek words from the sentences involved. One of the unhappy traits of the KJV is that it follows the TR at this point and contains all the dubious words of Acts 9:5-6.

C. 2 Peter 2:4

2 Peter 2:4 declares that God cast all the sinning angels down to hell and delivered them into either (1) **chains** of darkness, or (2) **pits** of darkness. The difference in the Greek text between the word for chains and the word for pits is only *a single Greek letter*. Chains is *sirais* while pits is *sirois*. Both are highly figurative expressions to indicate the surety of confinement because neither a literal chain or a literal pit could very adequately limit the movement of a spirit being!

The evidence for *chains* is found in P[72], K, P, Ψ , 049, 056, 0142 and the host of all the minuscules, lectionaries, some versions (Old Latin, Vulgate, Syriac, Coptic Bohairic, Armenian), plus such fathers as Ephraim, Didymus, Cyril, and a few later ones. The evidence for *pits* is limited to only four uncials, possibly one cursive, one Old Latin manuscript, the Coptic

Sahidic, Augustine, and a 5th century father. The critical texts frequently go with the **minority** reading (pits), supported by ﬡ , A, B, and C.

(1) *Antiquity* seems to rest with chains in the 3rd century Bodmer papyrus, the early versions, and several early fathers. (2) There is no question that *number* favors chains, as does the extent of the (3) *variety* evidenced in chains. This is seen in the widespread versions and the host of minuscules that come from every part of the world. (4) The *respectability* of each individual manuscript is difficult to apply--except that some give ﬡ , B, and C high marks, while others remember their abberations in Matt 27:49. (5) *Continuity* is greatly lacking in pits while it is considerable in chains. (6) Nothing in the surrounding *context* of these manuscripts would suggest any difficulty in either direction, and (7) the question of *reasonableness* is really not an issue either.

On the whole, I would choose chains as the best attested reading. The parallel passage in Jude 6 has a synonym for chains (*desmois,* bonds), which may argue that 2 Peter 2:4 might also have read chains. Others, however, might contend that pits is a more difficult reading than chains--which it may be. But a possible reconstruction of the problem may be that a slight copying mistake was made which changed an "a" to an "o," and that this error found its way into only a handful of manuscripts while the pure text was massively reproduced in hundreds of copies both before and after the error occurred in a few isolated copies.

III. TEXTUAL NOTES IN BIBLES

Many modern versions have notes on the Greek text in the margin or at the foot of the page.

These sometimes alert interested readers to possible textual variants. The most thorough of all such notes are found in the *New King James Version*. Some translations, however, merely translate and leave no rationale for the text they choose in problem areas. For example, in Luke 24:53 (the last verse of Luke), where the "blessing and praising" text occurs, several translations (ASV, RSV, TEV), choose only "blessing" and give no note to explain their choice. Others (Jerusalem Bible, NEB, NIV) give only "praising," again with no note in the text. The NASB gives an uncertain sound by translating the text as "praising," but appending a note that says it means literally "blessing." The KJV simply has both words, usually without a note, unless it comes in a study Bible. The NKJV also has "praising and blessing" with a textual note mentioning the fact that the Nestle's and the United Bible Societies' Greek texts omit the words "praising and."

Many translations, however, frequently *do* have notes on the text. One needs to carefully understand what such notes say and imply about the underlying Greek text. A good example would be the notes that come with John 7:53-8:11--the woman taken in adultery passage. The ASV says "Most of the ancient authorities omit John 7:53-8:11. Those which contain it vary much from each other." Actually the bulk of the Byzantine manuscripts (majority) *contain* the passage, so maybe the emphasis is on the word "ancient," and then it would be a close toss up. The RSV omits these twelve verses from their printed text, placing them in a footnote saying, "Other ancient authorities add 7:53-8:11 either here or at the end of this gospel or after Luke 21:38, with variations of the text." The omission of these verses from the text tells the story here. The mention of where the verses are placed is a smokescreen for the omission. The NEB follows the RSV, noting that the passage, "has no fixed place in our ancient witnesses," while putting the verses in *italics* in the text.

The NASB echoes the ASV by saying, "most of the ancient authorities omit" the passasge, and the TEV places the text in brackets with a note that declares, "many manuscripts and early translations do not have this passage . . . ." The NIV makes one of the boldest value judgments by its note right in an open space in the body of the text. It says, "The earliest and most reliable manuscripts do not have John 7:53-8:11." By contrast, the NKJV points out that the Nestle's and United Bible Societies' Greek texts bracket "7:53-8:11 as not original." But the note informatively adds, "They are present in over 900 mss" (mss = manuscripts).

Some might claim that in this Johannine passage Jesus seemed lax in condemning adultery. It is easy to see why some copyists might have wanted to leave it out. In fact, several uncial copies have that page torn out of their manuscript! The Nestle-UBS text has recently done an about face--and now claims the text in question should be included.

Be careful of such phrases as "earliest and best manuscripts" and so forth. These are either value judgments or ambiguous statements that could be misleading. In the following chapter, hints are given on how to evaluate modern translations. Six principles are suggested, and in this writer's mind, one translation consistently rises above the other modern versions when these criteria are applied.

IV.   FOR REVIEW AND DISCUSSION

1. Discuss the basic differences in methodology for textual criticism held by Westcott and Hort, Burgon, and advocates of the Textus Receptus.

2. Discuss in as much detail as possible the textual problems found in Matt 27:49, Acts 9:5-6, and 2 Peter 2:4. Can you clearly state what the problem of each passage is, as well as the possible solutions in each case?

3. Evaluate each of the three problems listed in #2 above using the suggested seven tests of truth for considering textual evidence. What are your conclusions in each case?

4. Discuss how textual notes in Bibles vary. Do you believe they are helpful or only open up new questions and problems for you? How about their value for the "average" Christian in the pew?

V.   FOR FURTHER READING AND DISCUSSION

Black, David Alan. *Rethinking New Testament Textual Criticism*. Grand Rapids: Baker Academic, 2002. 157 pp.

Bock, Darrell L., and Buist M. Fanning. *Interpreting the New Testament Text*. Wheaton: Crossway Books, 2006. 480 pp.

Borland, James A. "Re-Examining New Testament Textual Critical Principles and Practices Used to Negate Inerrancy." *Journal of the Evangelical Theological Society*. 25:4 (Dec. 1982): 499-506.

Burgon, John William. *The Last Twelve Verses of the Gospel According to S. Mark*. Evansville, IN: Sovereign Grace Book Club, 1959. 416 pp.

_____. *The Revised Revision.* Paradise, PA: Conservative Classics; reprinted, n.d.

Fee, Gordon D. "Rigorous or Reasoned Eclecticism— Which?" *Studies in New Testament Language and Text.* Ed. J. K. Elliot. Leiden: Brill, 1976. pp. 174-197.

_____. "The Textual Criticism of the New Testament." *The Expositor's Bible Commentary.* Ed. Frank Gaebelein. Grand Rapids: Zondervan, 1979. pp. 419-433.

Hodges, Zane C. "The Greek Text of the King James Version." *Bibliotheca Sacra.* 125 (Oct.-Dec., 1968): 334-345.

_____. "Rationalism and Contemporary New Testament Textual Criticism." *Bibliotheca Sacra.* 128 (Jan.-Mar., 1971): 27-35.

_____."The Woman Taken in Adultery (John 7:53-8:11): The Text." *Bibliotheca Sacra.* 136 (Oct.-Dec., 1979): 318-332.

King, Marchant A. "Should Conservatives Abandon Textual Criticism?" *Bibliotheca Sacra.* 130 (Jan.-Mar., 1973): 35-40.

Robinson, Maurice A. *The Conundrum of Acts 12:25.* 1996.

_____. *Preliminary Observations Regarding the Pericope Adulterae Based Upon Fresh Collations of Nearly All Continuous-Text Manuscripts and Over One Hundred Lectionaries.* 1998.

_____. *The Case for the Byzantine Textform A New Approach to "Majority Text" Theory.* Evangelical Theological Society papers, ETS-0430. 1991.

Robinson, Maurice A. and William G. Pierpont. *The New Testament in the Original Greek: Byzantine Textform.* Southborough, MA: Chilton Book Publishing, 2005.

Sitterly, C. F. and J. H. Greenlee. "Text and MSS of the NT." *The International Standard Bible Encyclopedia.* Ed. G. W. Bromiley. Grand Rapids: Eerdmans, 1979. V, 814-822.

15

HOW TO EVALUATE MODERN TRANSLATIONS

When a Christian looks for a Bible today, he is confronted with a veritable alphabet soup representing different translations--from the KJV, RSV, NEB, TEV, NASB, and NIV, to the NKJV. Most of these are available with the same variety of extra notes, references, study helps, maps, and concordances. So the real difference lies in the translation itself.

What things should a Christian consider when he looks for a new Bible? I would suggest that six points be considered: (1) the Translators, (2) the Text Used, (3) the Method of Translation, (4) the Theology, (5) the Type of Language and Style Used, and (6) the Biblical Tradition and Background of the Reader.

After looking carefully at these six items, it is my firm conviction that the New King James Version (NKJV) may indeed be the best translation for English-speaking Christians. The NKJV is clear and accurate without sacrificing majesty and readability. It also maintains and improves a tradition that has influenced the English-speaking world since 1611. Also, the NKJV is the only modern translation that does not either call into question or omit all or parts of

179

scores of New Testament verses. Yet, it provides the fullest set of footnotes dealing with textual matters to be found outside of a Greek New Testament itself. The reasons for this fortunate situation may be seen by briefly addressing the six considerations listed above.

I. THE TRANSLATORS

The translators of the NKJV were conservative, Bible-believing men of God who were experts in their fields. This could also be said of the NASB and NIV translators. In fact, some men have served on more than one of these different translation projects over the years.

The competence, recognized standing, and theological integrity of the scholars involved in the NKJV translation are beyond dispute. The choice of translators is of paramount importance for a translation, since the Word of God is being handled and must be approached with reverence and respect. It could not be said of some of the translators of the RSV, NEB, and TEV that they held to the view of the verbal and plenary inspiration of the Holy Scriptures. That is why some decline to use those translations and prefer instead the NKJV, NASB, and NIV. Yet, as important as the matter of the translators is, there are other serious considerations which set apart some modern versions from many of the others.

II. THE TEXT USED

A second consideration is the text from which a translation is made. Although there are relatively minor variations in the Hebrew text of the Old Testament, there are more radical differences in the available Greek manuscripts for the New

Testament. At this point, *all* modern English translations depart from the KJV textual heritage except one--the NKJV. The RSV,NEB,TEV, NASB, and NIV all use a text like the one currently published by the United Bible Societies, but first introduced by Westcott and Hort. It may be considered a radical text because it rejects the great majority of manuscripts while favoring only a small minority. This has resulted in many whole verses being deleted from these translations, while parts of many other verses are also missing. On the other hand, the NKJV follows the textual tradition underlying the 1611 King James Version. That text, known as the *Textus Receptus,* has some notable flaws of its own, but it is thought by this writer and many others to be superior to the abbreviated text used by the other versions.

For example, Mark 9:44, 46 do not exist in the NIV, RSV, NASB, TEV, and NEB. However, the overwhelming evidence based on antiquity, variety, continuity, and number is clearly in favor of the authenticity of those verses. Similarly, the familiar 58-word Lord's Prayer in Luke 11:2-4 is reduced to only 37 words in the RSV and NASB, and it shrinks to only 34 words in the NIV. The NKJV has 59 words.

But those omissions are slight compared to several much larger portions which are brought into serious question. Regarding Mark 16:9-20 and John 7:53-8:11, the NIV sets off these texts with blank space and a solid line across the page. Under that line in Mark a note reads, "The two most reliable early MSS omit Mark 16:9-20." The John passage has a similar note.

Not only are many verses and phrases omitted by some translators, but the biblical doctrine of inerrancy and verbal inspiration can also suffer. A case in point is Matthew 1:7 and 1:10. In the midst of the list of kings through whom Christ descended, the NASB tells its readers in a note that the Greek New Testament text has Asaph, a Psalmist, instead of good King Asa (v. 7); and Amos, a prophet, instead of King Amon (v. 10). This implies that Matthew made a mistake which was later corrected by scribes and copyists. That is the identical position taken by liberal textual critics who do not share the same high regard for inspiration claimed by the translators of the NASB.

III. THE METHOD OF TRANSLATION

A third point to consider is the method of translation employed by the translators. Some translations use a loose and free methodology, while others adhere more closely to the actual words of the Greek and Hebrew texts. The KJV, NASB, and NKJV would be examples of the latter, while the NIV and TEV, for example, often practice the former. It is universally agreed that idioms, figures of speech, and other irregular usages in language need careful handling in translation. However, to alter the words which God gave is a dangerous procedure. If God gave us His *verbally* inspired Word, then we ought not to translate it in a fashion that minimizes the actual words of the text. Not only the thoughts are important, but the very *words*--because precise thoughts can only rest upon clear, definite, and precise words.

Illustrations of this difference in methodology abound in every chapter. The NKJV is a mirror's reflection of the accuracy and care that went into the 1611 KJV, while the NIV, for example, takes more liberties with the text. Mark 3:20 may serve as a sample of this difference in methodology. The KJV and the NKJV both say that Jesus and his disciples were so busy "they could not so much as eat bread." That is a very accurate translation and makes perfect sense. Not only could they not stop to sit down to a regular meal, but they did not even have time to grab a piece of bread. The NASB changes "eat bread" to "eat a meal," with a note to indicate that bread would be more literal. The RSV, TEV, and NIV consider it sufficient to say simply that they had no time to eat, leaving out all mention of bread or a meal. There is no question about the existence of the word for bread in any Greek text.

But that is not the end of the liberties taken by the NIV and TEV in that very same verse. While the KJV, NKJV, ASV, NASB, and RSV all properly translate the Greek *autous* by "they," the TEV and NIV take the liberty to supply words into the text to explain just who "they" were who had no time to eat. Those two translations read, "Jesus and His disciples" (TEV), and "he and his disciples" (NIV). That clarification involved replacing God's word "they" with four other quite unauthorized and completely unnecessary words. The context is clear enough without *adding to* God's Word.

Another example of difference due to the same loose translation method of the NIV is found in Jesus' remark to His mother at the wedding feast in John 2:4. As is correct and true to the text, the KJV, followed by the ASV, NASB, and NKJV, all have Jesus calling His mother by the neutral term "woman." But the NIV and RSV, perhaps in an attempt to capture the flavor of the Greek case of direct address, add somewhat to the text. The NIV says "Dear Woman." That addition is not only unnecessary, but could give a totally wrong impression of Jesus' attitude toward His mother in this context. The NIV tends to add words, omit words, and to change some key words. Let the reader check 1 Cor 7:36 and he will find a wholesale interpretation inserted into the translation. Unhappily such liberties are not uncommon in the NIV.

IV. THE THEOLOGY

Every prospective translation also should be examined carefully for its theology. It is possible for a translation to espouse or advance, whether intentionally or not, some very poor theology. A case in point would be the rendering of the two final words of 1 Peter 2:2. These words are not found in the great majority of manuscripts and thus are not in the KJV or the NKJV, which are based on the *Textus Receptus*. The TEV indicates that by drinking the milk of the Word (Christian nuture) "you may grow up and be saved." Does salvation come through merely "growing up?"

An equally poor theological implication has been given by the NIV in Acts 2:38. There it says, "Repent and be baptized ... so that your sins may be forgiven." The TEV says, "... so that your sins will be forgiven." Is forgiveness actually dependent upon one's baptism? Naturally, that is a *theological* question. As such, only one's theology can determine the answer. In contrast, the KJV, RSV, NASB, and NKJV all use the proper neutral term "for" (instead of "so that") which can indicate either purpose or result. We must allow pastors, theologians, and other students of the Word to explain that difficult verse within the general context of the entire Scriptures. Acts 2:38 may be thought to teach baptismal regeneration, but if a translation pontificates on that narrow meaning, it may show a bias toward a particular theological viewpoint. It was perhaps due to this criticism that the NIV later changed this original translation of Acts 2:38.

With few exceptions, most modern translation committees are composed of scholars from several different denominations. This helps to guard against theological blind spots in the translation. Some Baptists might prefer the term "immerse" to translate the Greek word for baptizing, while Methodists and Presbyterians would prefer a more neutral term such as "baptize." The sectarian Jehovah's Witnesses' translation makes Christ a mere finite creature and the Mormon *Inspired Version,* translated by Joseph Smith, *added* some distinctly Mormon theology to the Book of Genesis. These problems are not generally encountered in most versions, but a trend toward looseness in translation can result in giving the reader a distorted doctrinal picture.

V. THE TYPE OF LANGUAGE AND STYLE USED

A fifth concern is that of language and style. A translation must use language that can be understood. As a result, most modern translations, including the NKJV, omit such forms as *thee, thou, wouldst, doeth,* and *saith,* although they are retained in the NASB in the Psalms and in passages addressed to God.

One feature of the NKJV that many appreciate is the capitalizing of nouns and pronouns referring to God. This helps the reader identify Christ, the Holy Spirit, and the Father much more easily. The NIV, TEV, and many others omit this practice. Along a different line, many of the newer versions (RSV, TEV, NIV) have gone to a paragraph format. It may be only a matter of taste, but it seems that printing each verse separately helps one find individual verses far more easily, certainly is an aid to congregational reading, and enhances memory work. Standard editions of the NKJV print the verses separately, while clearly indicating each new paragraph by a bold verse number. In addition, a boldface heading announces each new section. Another welcome improvement in the RSV, NASB, TEV, NIV, NKJV and others is the use of quotation marks.

In an attempt to use current language, some modern translations change important theological terms. For example, the NIV changes the word repentance to a "change of heart" in 2 Tim 2:25. The NKJV, on the other hand, makes it a practice to retain such words as *repentance, sanctification, redemption,* and *righteousness.* Changing these words can lead to misunderstanding rather than to clarification. What is meant by "a change of heart" may be open to speculation, while the meaning of the term repentance is generally known. "Change of heart" is a paraphrase.

VI. THE BIBLICAL TRADITION AND BACKGROUND OF THE READER

A final consideration is the biblical tradition and background of the reader. Most English-speaking Christians are somewhat familiar with the old King James Version. In an amazing fashion, the NKJV resembles that Bible which is loved and revered by so many, yet at the same time it breathes a new freshness and clarity throughout.

As noted earlier, all modern versions depart notably from the Greek text underlying the old KJV with the exception of the New King James Version. But that is not the only reason why they seem so different from the KJV. They have *sought* to be new, free, more colloquial, and modern. The NKJV, however, sought to be a proper revision of the KJV. Great care was taken to maintain the stylistic beauty, majesty, and power of the KJV, yet the translation reads with simplicity and clarity.

Many pastors and laymen alike have tried a simple test which relates to the biblical tradition and background with which they are familiar. When the NIV, TEV, and other modern translations are read, to some they just do not seem like the historic Bible. But when reading the NKJV a unique discovery is made. It not only seems like the Bible they are used to--it seems even better. It is easier to read and understand, yet it is beautiful, powerful, and majestic. That is just another reason why the New King James Version may indeed be the best English translation for most Christians.

VII. FOR REVIEW AND DISCUSSION

1. List and define the six criteria suggested for use in evaluating modern translations.
2. Obtain three or four different modern translations, then try to apply each of the six criteria to those translations. Which points require outside research, and which can be discovered within the pages of each Bible?
3. Were you surprised by some of the things you learned about the different versions in this

chapter? What areas may have concerned you the most?

4. Do you feel that the points made about the different versions were soundly based, or did you react negatively to some areas of discussion? Why or why not?

5. Do you have strong feelings about one or more modern versions? Which ones, and why?

6. Do you feel that the information presented in this chapter will help you to better evaluate modern translations in the future? If so, how?

VIII.   FOR FURTHER READING AND RESEARCH

Bruce, Frederick Fyvie. *The English Bible: A History of Translations from the Earliest English Versions to the New English Bible.* Rev. ed. New York: Oxford, 1970.

Carson, Donald A. *The King James Version Debate: A Plea for Realism.* Grand Rapids: Baker, 1979. 128 pp.

Dennett, Herbert. *A Guide to Modern Versions of the New Testament.* Chicago: Moody, 1966. xiv + 142.

Ewert, David. *From Ancient Tablets to Modern Translations.* Grand Rapids: Zondervan, 1983. 284 pp.

Fuller, Russell T. "Choosing a Translation of the Bible." *Journal for Biblical Manhood and Womanhood.* 10:2 (Fall, 2005): 56-65.

Grudem, Wayne. "Are the Criticisms of the TNIV Bible Really Justified? An Interaction with Craig Blomberg, Darrell Bock, Peter Bradley, D. A. Carson, and Bruce Waltke." *Journal for Biblical Manhood and Womanhood.* 7:2 (Fall, 2002) 18-52.

Grudem, Wayne and Grant R. Osborne. "Do Inclusive-Language Bibles Distort Scripture?" *Christianity Today.* 41:12 (October 27, 1997): 26-39.

Grudem, Wayne with Jerry Thacker. *Why Is My Choice of a Bible Translation So Important?* Louisville: Council on Biblical Manhood and Womanhood, 2005.

Hodges, Zane C. "The Text of the New Testament and Modern Translations." *Christianity Today.* (June 22, 1973): 6-10.

Kubo, Sakae and Walter Specht. *So Many Versions?* Grand Rapids: Zondervan, 1975. 244 pp.

Makkai, Valerie Becker. "Gendered Language and Bible Translation." *Journal for Biblical Manhood and Womanhood.* 6:1 (Spring, 2001): 27-30.

Owens, Pamela Dean. "Bible Translator and Language Preservation." *The Bible Translator.* 57:1 (January, 2006): 1-10.

Poythress, Vern S. and Wayne A. Grudem. *The TNIV and the Gender-Neutral Bible Controversy.* Nashville: Broadman and Holman, 2004. xxv + 494.

Price, James. D. *King James Onlyism: A New Sect.* Chattanooga, TN: James D. Price, 2006. xvi + 658.

Stein, David E. S. "God's Name in a Gender Sensitive Jewish Translation." *The Bible Translator.* 58:3 (July, 2007): 105-110.

Taylor, Richard. "The Modern Debate Concerning the Greek Textus Receptus." *Biblical Viewpoint.* 8:1 (April, 1974): 60-69.

Torode, Sam. "The Abolition of Man." *World.* 17:26 (July 7/13, 2002): 42-44.

Wegner, Paul D. *The Journey from Texts to Translations: The Origin and Development of the Bible.* Grand Rapids: Baker Academic, 2004. 462 pp.

APPENDIX

THE SYNOPTIC PROBLEM

APPENDIX

THE SYNOPTIC PROBLEM

I. UNDERSTANDING THE SYNOPTIC PROBLEM

There are three synoptic Gospels--Matt, Mark, and Luke. Each broadly tells the story of Jesus in the same way, covering the same ground from the baptism to the crucifixion and resurrection. The great Galilean ministry is prominent in each of the synoptics. Synoptic means to view similarly. Yet each presents a particular viewpoint molded for a certain audience. On the other hand, John is *not* a synoptic Gospel. He omits the Galilean ministry and instead concentrates on the Judean ministry in chapters 2-3, 5, and 7-20.

The problem that presented itself to some critics was how Matt, Mark, and Luke could be so similar in their overall presentations, quite frequently even using identical Greek words and phrases, and yet include or omit some material that one of the others used. Why, for example, do only Matt and Luke have birth narratives? Why do some of the details of various miracles differ? Where did each writer get his information? Were any of the writers dependent on each other, or did they write independently of one another? What can account for the frequent use of identical wording by two or more of the synoptic writers? Did Matt, Mark, or Luke use any common sources, or did any two of the writers have access to a source the third writer did not have? Many possible answers have been suggested, some of which are briefly explained in the following section.

II. SUGGESTED ANSWERS TO THE SYNOPTIC PROBLEM

A. The Common Original Theory

As far back as the late 1700's there were some who taught that Matthew may have written an early Gospel in Aramaic (not Greek), and that all other Gospels drew upon that common source-- including Matthew himself when he wrote our Greek Matt. This theory has little support today and rests upon no literary evidence of any such "original" Aramaic Gospel.

B. The Many Fragments Theory

In the early 1800's a theory was developed which suggested that many smaller fragments about Christ's life circulated, and that Matt, Mark, and Luke may have used these "common" sources when composing their own Gospels. These many different fragments could hardly explain the synoptics' great similarity in the order of events covered, and it would not guarantee that their very wording at times should be so alike. Furthermore, these many fragments have somehow disappeared and left no trace--not even a forwarding address.

C. The Mutual Dependence Theory

Numerous individuals over the centuries have suggested that the second Gospel writer drew from the first, and that the third writer relied on both of the earlier two. Every conceivable order of the three was suggested (there are six possibilities). Although, out of favor as a theory today, the suggested order of Mark, followed by Matt, and then Luke edged toward the development of the two document view.

D. The Two Document Theory

The basic two document theory or hypothesis is another attempt to solve the synoptic problem. It holds that Mark was written first, and that a second early document, commonly called Q (from the German *Quelle* = source), contained additional information about Jesus. The theory holds that Matt and Luke copied materials from both Mark and Q and that their actions account for the similarities. As popular as this theory is, several important questions remain unanswered. (1) Can it be proven that Mark predated Matt and Luke? (2) Would Matt and Luke have been such plagiarists, or so dependent on Mark that they had to copy almost verbatim so much of Mark? (3) Why did Luke omit some large sections of Mark? (4) Why is there no record or copy of the supposed Q document? (5) What is to account for the many differences between Matt and Luke if they both used identical sources?

An additional criticism of the two document approach is that it became in vogue just when the theory of human evolution was being popularized (later 1800's). The Mark-Q theory is one of *literary development and evolution*--from the simplest to the more complex. It is held that Mark, the brief 16 chapter account was expanded into Matt's 28 and Luke's 24 chapters. Because of the inability of the two document theory to explain some of the above questions, especially #5, Burnett Streeter proposed a *four* document hypothesis in his study of the origins of the four Gospels in 1924.

E.   Streeter's Four Document Theory

Feeling the inadequacy of the Mark-*Q* theory, but building upon it, B. H. Streeter proposed that Matt and Luke each used an additional source peculiar to their own Gospel. Matt's accessory he termed **M**, while he called Luke's supplement **L**.

M, for example, would supply those portions of Matt that could not be obtained from either Mark or *Q*--namely certain Judaistic sections. But Streeter held that M, L, and *Q*, overlapped somewhat, so that their contents could not be packaged so neatly. The basic priority of Mark and the existence of *Q* are still accepted by many critical scholars today.

F.   Form Criticism

Form criticism, or *formgeschichte* (form history), is a more modern statement of the many fragments theory. It holds that the Gospels developed by combining, recombining, and editing different accounts of early traditions about Jesus. These accounts, it is held, are from various literary types or genres--such as (1) tales (miracles), (2) legends (of saints), (3) birth accounts, (4) sayings, (5) myths (baptism, temptation, transfiguration), (6) paradigms (short narratives), (7) passion stories, and so forth.

A major criticism of form criticism is that it generally assumes the forms to be myth or legend without prior argument. The mere *form* of a story, however, cannot prove either the truth or falsity of its contents. Truth can be conveyed in prose, poetry, or parable. Unhappily, many of the leading critics behind *formgeschichte* (Bultmann, for example), have had trouble believing that the New Testament could be trusted in what it said about Jesus.

G. The Oral Tradition Theory

A final proposal that seems to fall short of being a proper explanation for the synoptic problem is the oral tradition theory. It was an attempt to explain the problem apart from any references to literary dependence. This theory maintains that the synoptic Gospels were composed on the common basis of a circulating oral tradition. This oral tradition could possibly explain the similarity in the order of events recounted in Matt, Mark, and Luke, and might even explain some of the affinity of verbal expression as well. However, this theory by itself fails to consider all of the evidence and does not even demand that Matt, Mark, and Luke were inspired by God. The following viewpoint is presented in an effort to strike a good balance with the evidence of the problem, although it is only mentioned in outline.

SYNOPTIC RELATIONSHIPS

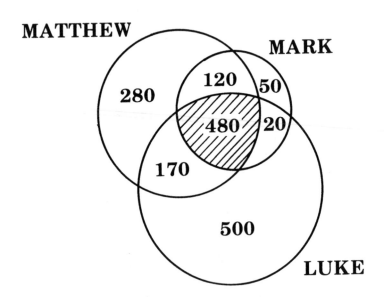

	Differences	Agreements
MATTHEW	42%	58%
MARK	7%	93%
LUKE	59%	41%
JOHN	92%	8%

INTERPRETATION: *Mark has 678 verses. Only about 50 of those are unique to Mark. He shares 480 with **both** Matt and Luke, and another 120 with Matt only, and another 20 with Luke only. Thus Mark demonstrates differences only 7%, while showing agreements 93% of the time.*

III. A BALANCED SOLUTION TO THE SYNOPTIC PROBLEM

A balanced solution to the synoptic problem seems possible for a Bible-believer who considers all aspects of the question. Certainly, as Luke 1:1 testifies, there were some literary documents in circulation, and an oral tradition must have been passed on by the Apostles and others. But one must not forget that the Apostles themselves were eyewitnesses to many of the events in the life of Christ, and that the Holy Spirit inspired the very words that they wrote. These last two points are not given much attention by many critical scholars, but are nonetheless a matter of utmost importance to the Fundamentalist. Not only that, but these issues help one to make a lot more sense of the whole problem as well.

A. The Writers Were Early Witnesses

Matt and John were disciples of Jesus and stood as eyewitnesses to most of what Jesus said and did during His public ministry. Mark was very close to both Peter and Paul (1 Peter 5:13; 2 Tim 4:11), while Luke accompanied Paul into Palestine where he could consult eyewitnesses for several years (Acts 21:8-26:32). Thus, none of the three synoptic writers was without important first-hand sources. Peter, whom it is thought aided Mark, was certainly an outstanding testimony of the words and events. Luke probably consulted a number of the early Apsotles and may have interviewed even Mary herself before writing the account of the births of John the Baptist and of Jesus.

B. The Writers Probably Followed an Oral Tradition

The story of Jesus was frequently told in terms of His baptism, then His preaching, teaching and healing in Galilee, and finally His passion in Jerusalem. Peter's testimony to Cornelius' household follows this outline (Acts 10:37-43), as does the brief account of Paul's sermon at Antioch of Pisidia (Acts 13:23-31). Mark's Gospel follows this oral testimony, as do both Matt and Luke. That is a large part of the reason those three books are grouped together and termed the synoptics.

The oral tradition may account for more than just coincidences in subject matter. As material is repeated over and over again it frequently takes on a set form in its very words. For instance, if I asked a group of persons to repeat independently of each other what they could remember of the story of "The Three Little Pigs," such words as first, second, third, straw, sticks, brick, chimney, pig, wolf, hair of my chinny chin chin, etc. would be common to each oral presentation. The synoptics as well, could have benefited from the common repetition of the story of Jesus--even to the extent that many words and whole phrases would become common to each of their various written compositions.

C. The Writers May Have Used Short Written Accounts

Luke mentions that there were a number of written accounts of Jesus' life and ministry (Luke 1:1). Although we do not know whether he may have used such sources, it remains a distinct possibility. That such written sources were not inspired is beyond question, but such does not in

MATTHEW   *KING*   JEWS

LION

Key Verses: Sixteen times Matt points to a fulfillment of the Hebrew Scriptures--"This was done that it might be fulfilled." Matt 1:22; 2:14, 17, 23; 4:14; 5:18; 8:17; 12:17; 13:14, 35; 21:4; 24:34; 26:54, 56; 27:9, 35.

MARK   *SERVANT*   ROMANS

OX

Key Verse: **10:45.** "For even the Son of Man did not come to be served, but to serve, and to give His life a ransom for many."

LUKE   *SON OF MAN*   GREEKS

MAN

Key Verse: **19:10.** "For the Son of Man has come to seek and to save that which was lost."

JOHN   *SON OF GOD*   ALL MANKIND

EAGLE

Key Verse: **20:31.** "But these are written that you may believe that Jesus is the Christ, the Son of God, and that believing you may have life in His name.

any way compromise Luke's integrity, since he selected his material and wrote under the guidance of the Holy Spirit (2 Peter 1:21). If Luke occasionally came across some written accounts, then the possibility is that Matt and Mark may have as well. However, their use of any such materials would have been within the bounds of the doctrine of inspiration to which we turn next.

D. The Writers Were Verbally Inspired

As discussed earlier in chapter 10, each of the writers of the New Testament was born along by the miraculous work of the Holy Spirit which assured that the literary product was verbally and plenarily inspired and wholly without error (2 Tim 3:16; 2 Peter 1:21). Although this fact is somewhat ignored or downplayed by critics, it is all-important to one who believes the Bible to be the Word of God.

Each writer pursued his own purpose and theme for his intended audience. Many times there was a great concurrence among the three synoptic writers, and at other points their divergencies are evident. Each writer was led to achieve the goal placed in his mind by the Holy Spirit. There are no contradictions or conflicts among them, just three separate viewpoints given expression--but all under the superintending work of God, the Author in back of the authors.

IV. FOR REVIEW AND DISCUSSION

1.   What are the three synoptic Gospels, and why are they so called?
2.   What is the synoptic problem? Be as complete in your answer as possible.

3. Be able to list and give the essence of the answers men have suggested for the synoptic problem. What criticisms could be leveled against each of these inadequate views?
4. What four areas need to be considered in formulating a balanced approach to the synoptic problem? How important are each of these points in answering the question?

V. FOR FURTHER READING AND RESEARCH

Black, David Alan and David R. Beck. *Rethinking the Synoptic Problem*. Grand Rapids: Baker, 2001.

Carson, D. A. "Matthew." *The Expositor's Bible Commentary*. Ed. F. E. Gaebelein. Grand Rapids: Zondervan, 1984. VIII, 11-17.

Dyer, Charles H. "Do the Synoptics Depend on Each Other?" *Bibliotheca Sacra*. 138 (July-Sept., 1981): 230-245.

Evans, Craig A. "Sorting Out the Synoptic Problem: Why an Old Approach Is Still Best." *Reading the Gospels Today*. Ed. Stanley E. Porter. Grand Rapids: Eerdmans, 2004. pp. 1-26.

Goodacre, Mark S. *The Case Against Q: Studies in Markan Priority and the Synoptic Problem*. Harrisburg, PA: Trinity Press, 2002.

Guthrie, Donald. *New Testament Introduction*. 3rd Ed. Downers Grove, IL: InterVarsity, 1970. pp. 121-236.

Harrison, Everett F. *Introduction to the New Testament*. Rev. ed. Grand Rapids: Baker, 1973. pp. 142-166.

Hendricksen, William. *Exposition of the Gospel According to Matthew*. Grand Rapids: Baker, 1973. pp. 6-76.

Kümmel, Werner Georg. *Introduction to the New Testament*. 14th Rev. ed. Trans. A. J. Mattill, Jr. Nashville: Abingdon, 1966. pp. 31-60.

204 A General Introduction to the New Testament

Linnemann, Eta. *Is there a Synoptic Problem? Rethinking the Literary Dependence of the First Three Gospels.* Trans. R. W. Yarbrough. Grand Rapids, Baker, 1992.

Longstaff, Thomas R. W. and Page A. Thomas. *The Synoptic Problem: A Bibliography, 1716-1988.* Macon, GA: Mercer University, 1988. xxviii + 235.

McKnight, Scott and Matthew C. Williams. *The Synoptic Gospels: An Annotated Bibliography.* Grand Rapids: Baker, 2000.

Stein, Robert H. *The Synoptic Problem: An Introduction.* Grand Rapids: Baker, 1987.

Stonehouse, Ned Bernard. *Origins of the Synoptic Gospels.* Grand Rapids: Eerdmans, 1963.

Streeter, Burnett Hillman. *The Four Gospels: A Study of Origins.* New York: Macmillan, 1925. xiv + 622.

Thiessen, Henry Clarence. *Introduction to the New Testament.* Grand Rapids: Eerdmans, 1943. pp. 101-129.

Thomas, Robert L., Ed. *Three Views on the Origins of the Synoptic Gospels.* Grand Rapids: Kregel, 2002

Wenham, John William. *Redating Matthew, Mark & Luke: A Fresh Assault on the Synoptic Problem.* Downers Grove, IL: InterVarsity, 1992.

Westcott, Brooke Foss. *An Introduction to the Study of the Gospels.* 5th ed. London: Macmillan, 1875. pp. 161-208.

INDEX OF NAMES

INDEX OF SCRIPTURES

INDEX OF SUBJECTS